AIM THE STARS REACH THE MOON

How to Coach Your Life to Material and Spiritual Success

CONOR PATTERSON

DEDICATION

To my parents, Dixi and Mike Patterson

Copyright © 2005 O Books
O Books is an imprint of John Hunt Publishing Ltd., The Bothy, Deershot
Lodge, Park Lane, Ropley, Hants, SO24 0BE, UK
office@johnhunt-publishing.com
www.O-books.net

Distribution in:
UK
Orca Book Services
orders@orcabookservices.co.uk
Tel: 01202 665432 Fax: 01202 666219 Int. code (44)

USA and Canada
NBN
custserv@nbnbooks.com
Tel: 1 800 462 6420 Fax: 1 800 338 4550

Australia
Brumby Books
sales@brumbybooks.com
Tel: 61 3 9761 5535 Fax: 61 3 9761 7095

New Zealand
Peaceful Living
books@peaceful-living.co.nz
Tel: 64 7 57 18105 Fax: 64 7 57 18513

Singapore
STP
davidbuckland@tlp.com.sg
Tel: 65 6276 Fax: 65 6276 7119

South Africa
Alternative Books
altbook@global.co.za
Tel: 27 011 792 7730 Fax: 27 011 972 7787

Text: © Conor Patterson 2005

Design: BookDesign™, London, UK

ISBN 1 905047 27 4

All rights reserved. Except for brief quotations in critical articles or reviews, no part of this book may be reproduced in any manner without prior written permission from the publishers.

The rights of Conor Patterson as author have been asserted in accordance with the Copyright, Designs and Patents Act 1988.

A CIP catalogue record for this book is available from the British Library.

www.lifecoach.gb.com

Printed in the USA by Maple-Vail Manufacturing Group

AIM FOR THE STARS REACH THE MOON

How to Coach Your Life to Material and Spiritual Success

CONOR PATTERSON

BOOKS

WINCHESTER UK
NEW YORK USA

About The Book

IF you are looking for another book full of things to do that might lead to personal improvement, then please return this book to its shelf. Rather than just containing ideas and education, the book you are reading gives precise techniques that have proven to totally transform the lives of real people in the real world. By using the techniques, you will not just get an exciting emotional boost, you will begin leading an empowered life where everything is massively developed, from the depths of your spiritual fulfillment to the top of your financial success. These techniques have been entrusted to me by some of the world's leading visionaries, coaches and teachers. I have served them up in a direct format that can immediately start improving your health, wealth and joy. By teaching these techniques over the years, I have developed a unique way of delivering them which I call *Enhance*. It is through this system that so many of my clients have directly benefited from the wealth of knowledge passed on to me by such luminaries as Richard Bandler, Paul McKenna, Anthony Robbins, Jagadish Parikh, Masaru Emoto, John de Ruiter, Uri Geller, Barbara Wren, Swami Chandresh, Anita Boardman, Kate Edmonds, Mira, Ramesh Balsekar, and Mark Tyrell.

The action of opening this book is the first of many that will empower your life forever ... with one condition. That condition is that you continue to read and apply the techniques and attitudes described within these pages. In doing so, your life may not only advance greatly in terms of finance, relationships and career, but also in the enjoyment of your life. You have probably already realized that the most important thing in life is not what happens to you but how you experience what happens to you. Your life can so easily become filled with more joy, more satisfaction, and more contentment. You do not have to settle for less, but rather you can settle for more. It is in those moments of being who you truly are and seeing yourself moving into action that life really lights up. This book is an invitation to leave behind an ordinary life forever. I hope you accept it. The choice is yours …

About The Author

Conor Patterson is a British life coach renowned for his empowering insights. His work is to inspire people to recognize their nature as God and thereby better their lives. He has worked with film stars and multimillionaires as well as psychiatric patients and the homeless. Conor developed the content of *Aim For the Stars, Reach the Moon* after fourteen years of research around the world studying with living teachers.

Born in 1973, he studied media and was director of his own computer animation company. In 1997, he left everything to search for that "something more", discovering that it is always within us, around us and available to us. He then met his wife, Julie, whom he has been with for eight years. Returning to the UK, he retrained and started the personal development company, Heart in Action.

He has been personally trained and licensed by Dr Richard Bandler, co-inventor of Neuro-Linguistic Programming. Conor says of Richard, "He has shown me how to facilitate true and lasting improvements to the lives of other people." Conor also holds a two-year Diploma in Life Coaching from Newcastle College, a three-year BSc in Media Communications from Bradford University, and a Certificate in Personal Development from Sussex Career Services.

He likes to eat tuna, sunbathe and play tennis (but never at the same time).

See www.lifecoach.gb.com for more details.

Contents

Acknowledgments	x
Introduction	xi

Part 1 – Experience Yourself
1.	Experience God	2
2.	Experience Uniqueness	15
3.	Experience the Whole Range of Yourself	24

Part 2 – Know Yourself
4.	Know When to Accept and When to Act	42
5.	Know What is Important to You	58
6.	Know your Boundaries	65
7.	Know your Fears	74

Part 3 – Empower Yourself
8.	Empower Your Mind	90
9.	Empower Your Body	99
10.	Empower Your Emotions	113

Part 4 – Guide Yourself
11.	Guide to Your Heart	124
12.	Guide to Success	134
13.	Guide to the Work You Love	150
14.	Guide to an Empowering Relationship	164
15.	Guide to Creating Abundance in Your Life	179

Epilogue	189
Resources	190

Acknowledgements

THIS book came into being as a result of using techniques to empower my own life and the lives of others. I wish to thank the many people that have assisted me in my life journey. I consider you all to be dear friends. Thanks in particular go to Julie, my beautiful partner, who has continually believed in a vision that keeps getting bigger and stronger. Thanks also to my siblings, Brendan, Siobhan, Kerry, Jamie and Grainne who have been a wellspring of understanding. Deep gratitude goes to my parents for inviting me to this planet. Thanks to my publisher, John Hunt, for seeing the scope of this work and for helping the text to develop. Thanks to Kate Edmonds for giving freely of her time to bring me into a greater place. Respect and gratitude to Richard Bandler who communicated the building blocks some of my techniques use. Thanks also to Paul McKenna for inspiring people to grow. My gratitude goes to Alan Jacobs for mentoring me on the path of authorship. Thanks also to those who have helped with Heart in Action in the last year, especially Juliet Kearns, Mora McIntyre and Mervyn Wright.

Three years ago I was cleaning floors. Now I run one of the biggest personal development companies in the UK. I could not have done this alone. Thank you to everyone I have met along the way who has contributed something positive to this work. Finally, my eternal gratitude and love goes to the greatest teachers: the plants, the elements and the stars.

Introduction

DURING my studies of famous people, I came across two very distinguished household names whose fathers both used the same phrase. They used to say to their young sons, "Aim for the stars and you might reach the moon." I love this phrase since personal development is exactly like this. To raise life up to a new improved level we have to stretch our vision of what is possible. While we may not reach exactly where we aim, we will certainly reach higher than if we never aimed at all. And you never know, you may reach the stars …

By reading and applying this book you can expect to have more energy, more relaxation, greater fulfillment, better relationships, a stronger self-image, a greater sense of time to do what you love, and a more satisfying experience of work. Using this book, you can relax as life improvement happens easily and simply. You can watch as your life transforms into something very invigorating and wondrous.

Each chapter has a very simple and quick exercise that can bring profound, beneficial and lasting changes to your life. After each exercise are a few frequently asked questions and answers. The questions and answers relate directly to the subject at hand and have been transcribed from my talks, workshops, seminars, and retreats. At the end a very personal story taken from one of my coaching clients is included. These stories illustrate how the techniques in the chapter have been used and how they worked for real people.

The book begins with a return to your true nature, and reveals that within you is the self same power that creates all that you can see around you. Put simply, God is within you. We then progress to self-knowledge as you get to really know yourself. Once you know yourself, you can progress to the third part, which is empowerment. Here you will learn many tools and techniques to quickly improve the functioning of your mind, emotions and body. Finally, you will receive a number of guides that you can use for yourself to manifest whatever you wish for in your life. Whether you are looking for spiritual fulfillment, more money, easier relationships, greater health, or any other form of improvement to life's riches, then I congratulate you for taking the first step.

As you read *Aim for the Stars*, you can build the faith and confidence that allow huge changes to happen very quickly in your life. You can do this simply by understanding that when changes occur you will experience a heightening of awareness. When you befriend this heightened awareness, whether or not is seems to be fear or excitement, then when the changes inevitably take place in your life you can facilitate them without disturbance.

PART 1

EXPERIENCE YOURSELF

Experience is the most important aspect of life. What you experience defines what is real for you. When your experience expands, so does your perception of what is possible. If you, for just one moment, can have an experience of being totally whole, that experience could change your reality forever. The start of this book is an opportunity to go into your own power in a way that can have far-reaching benefits for the rest of your life.

1

Experience God

"Mankind has lost its way and seems hardly to know or care. But one freedom remains, and it is the call of the heart to find a new beginning; to create for ourselves a sheltering place where we might make again a cathedral for the soul that requires no great edifice of sculptured stone but rather a surrender to the still small voices within us."
Brian Keenan

"In union there is strength."
Aesop

"Nothing is life is more wonderful than faith."
Sir William Osler

"Let your life lightly dance on the edges of Time like dew on the tip of a leaf."
Tagore

You can be whole whenever you wish

HAVE you ever had an event in your life that made you feel whole? Did anything happen to you where you experienced a kind of homecoming that made you feel like you are truly yourself? It may have been when you were with someone you love very deeply, or when you accomplished something great in your life. Perhaps you experienced an uplifting sense of your true ability. These experiences that you have had are an intimate encounter with God. Before I go on any further, let me explain what I mean by God. God is not a man with a beard sitting on a cloud judging your every action. In fact "he" is not even a "he". God is genderless and formless. God is the life force that flows through and within every single one of us. To put God outside of oneself is a terrible and costly mistake. To believe God is only within you is just as disastrous. God exists within you and within every other creature, object and action, *equally and unconditionally*. It is very important to become aware that God has always been within you, that you are God as much as God is you, and that everything else in the universe is in the same position. Whether alive or inanimate, God is the power that connects everything in the universe together. God is known under many names, each just as valid: Love, Kindness, Unity, Tao, Brahma, Allah, Jehovah, Higher Consciousness, Life Force, Eternal Nature, Invisible Power, Formless Substance, and so on. But most importantly, God is wholeness. There is nothing lacking in God.

This book is an opportunity to embrace the infinite power of God within you. You can do this without having to change your religious beliefs or adopt new ones. Even if you cannot relate to what I am saying right now, this book can lead you into an awareness of what God is. By applying a few quick and easy techniques, you can demonstrate the immense power that you have available to you on a day-to-day basis.

Most people wait for something in their lives to tell them they are whole before they experience it. They feel fragmented or somehow separate from life until something wonderful happens and then they suddenly feel whole again. For example, you may feel isolated and unhappy until a beautiful person comes into your life and sweeps you off your feet. You feel thrilled and a sense of wholeness returns to you. This sense of wholeness is actually *inside* you always, but the experience of loving another puts you in touch with it. Imagine what would happen if you didn't have to wait for the right circumstances before you felt whole in your life. What could you do with your life if you knew that you were whole and that you didn't need anything to produce that feeling? What could you accomplish?

YOUR NATURE AS GOD

EACH of us is born into this world totally whole. As babies, we made little distinction between who was separate from us and who was the same as us. As we grew from babies into children, we learnt to distinguish between "you" and "I". We learnt how other people were different to us and separate from us. We learnt that objects were outside of us, and not just an extension of our body.

This was an essential part of growing up. We needed to know about differences in the world so that we could explore it safely. For example, we needed to know the difference between the door and the wall to avoid painful collisions. In relating to others, differences are essential so that we can come together to form a relationship. Distinction between what is your own property and someone else's is useful (if a little confusing when very young!) The learning of separation and differences was entirely natural.

But something went wrong to most of the people I know. The understanding that they are separate became their only reality. The experience of being whole was abandoned as they explored the world and found out about all the fascinating things within it. It is true that differences do exist on the surface of the world. Objects, people and property are all identified by their contrasting natures. But when we dig a little deeper within ourselves, we find that deep down, everyone is *the same*. Deep down everyone is whole.

We came into this world whole and nothing but our perception has changed since then. We are still that wholeness. That wholeness is God alive inside of us. As we grew up, we got caught in the amazing world of difference and separation, thereby forgetting that we are indeed whole. This forgetfulness has all sorts of damaging consequences. For example, behind most addictive behavior is the desire to be whole. When one accepts that they are whole already, they no longer need to get wholeness by attaining something outside of them. In the same way, a constant striving for material goods can take away the enjoyment from life. Again, behind this kind of striving is an underlying need to be whole. When you recognize that you *are* whole, then you will infinitely multiply the choices available to you during this lifetime. When you are not trapped by urgent strivings to find wholeness, then you have more power to use your energy to accomplish whatever you truly love. Remember that God is wholeness. You know when you have accepted that God is within you when you no longer need to find wholeness in the world through another person, your work or a substance. No event or thing in the world can give you the wholeness that you really are. To be aware of this, is to know that God is your nature. This awareness of God as your nature is the source of the great power that will work wonders in your life.

When something is natural to you, you can do that thing without thought or effort. You can speak English easily because you have grown up speaking it. You have English "inside you" and can therefore use the language in the world to produce results. For example, you can speak to people without thinking about how you do that. You don't have to "do" English anymore because you have already learnt it and it can now flow spontaneously from you. In the same way, recognizing that you are God can become second nature.

When you realize that you are God, then the wholeness you will experience can be used in the world to produce results. You can create health in the body, or make money more easily, or work in a job you love. All these worldly accomplishments can be achieved with little effort simply by honoring your nature as God. You can do this because:

When you *are* God, then you are able to bring God into the world.

Things that once seemed separate from you can be attracted towards you by the very fact that you are acting as God. Since God exists in everything, when you *are* God you are able to bring another part of "you" towards yourself. For example, when you live as God, then you can reconnect with a damaged part of your body and listen to what it needs, respond to it and make it healthy. Or you could bring money toward you that before seemed separate from you and out of reach. Once you live as God, you need not struggle in a job that you hate while searching for a feeling of wholeness. Instead, you can experience wholeness in the present moment, and then move into doing work that you truly enjoy. Living with a recognition that God is "inside you" is the first step to releasing a massively benevolent force in your life. We can better understand this recognition of God being within you by imagining that life is a flower …

YOU'VE GOT TO BE KIDDING – LIFE IS NOT A FLOWER!

LOOK, just imagine for a moment that life is a flower. As you know, a flower has a stem leading to a circle of petals at the top. Imagine that you are one petal within that flower. You can sit at the top of the flower and look over at all the other petals. You know that you are different to the other petals – you are unique, and separate from them. You are conscious of being different to the other petals but not of how you are the same as them. Now, imagine what would happen if you took your awareness to the stem of the flower and realized that you were in fact the source of the flower. Imagine the confusion for start! You are both the stem and a petal, both the source of the flower and a unique expression of it. But if you could accept this, imagine what it would be like returning your awareness to being a petal once again. How do you think your perspective would have changed? Would you still believe yourself to be separate from the other petals? Or would you recognize that you are actually the same as them, and at the *very same time* different to them. It is not necessary for you to understand this paradox now, simply to become a little more open to the fact that you are separate as a person *and* whole as God.

When you are reconnected with your nature as God, you experience a tremendous silence, peace and homecoming. When you are totally immersed in this experience, it will remind you of something that many people are forgetting: we are essentially *one*.

COURAGE TO BE WHOLE

AS you begin to experience your nature as God, you will notice that the world seems to change around you. When you are aware that you are whole, you relate differently to things and people. Life is uplifted to a new level of appreciation and wonderment. Passion can flow easily into your life and wonderful things spontaneously happen. The pressure to get a lover or a heap of money to make you feel whole is gone. You are free to do whatever you wish with your life because your sense of God is guaranteed forever. No matter how alone or how poor you are, you will experience wholeness. Therefore, being in good company and making lots of money is easy and satisfying. Desiring to have the things of the world is a natural move towards growth and improvement. This is exactly how God flows in the world: towards growth and improvement. How else could all these perfected forms of life come into existence had not the flow of God been towards growth and improvement?

As you experience God more and more in your life, you will notice how it may be a little tricky to communicate what is happening to those nearest and dearest to you. They may be perplexed as to how you are calm and centered inside no matter what is happening in your life. They may even try to deter you from being like that because it makes them feel uncomfortable. Explaining the sheer bliss of God to those that are not aware of it can be a challenge. People can generally only appreciate something when they have experienced it for themselves. A story illustrates this:

> One sunny day, a goldfish called Sam was enjoying a swim with all the other fish in their pond. The fish had often seen the shimmering light streaming down into the pond from above, but none had ventured beyond the surface. Some fish said it was dangerous, others said it was not important, but none had actually looked there. Now, Sam being a very curious fish, decided that he would find out for himself, what lay beyond the shimmering light. He swam to the bottom of the pond, and then shot swiftly upwards so that he could push through the surface and catch a glimpse of what was there.
>
> Sam was utterly amazed by what he could see above the water. There in front of him was a world he never knew existed. He could see huge trees, people talking to each another, and a big blue sky that seemed to stretch on forever into the distance. He could also feel the heat of the dazzling sun, which was far hotter than anything he had ever felt before. He was astonished. Although he was a little short of breath, he suddenly had a wonderful feeling. He felt that his life would never be the same again. His eyes were opened to another part of existence that he had previously known nothing about.

Diving back down into the pond, Sam quickly looked for the other fish to tell them what had happened. "I saw huge plants, and a hot yellow ball, and creatures that walked on two legs," he said excitedly. Most of the fish were unimpressed. They did not believe the tales because they had no proof. Other fish were interested but could not understand what Sam was talking about because they had no reference to it. Only one of the other fish, a small white one called Lizzie, listened to Sam intently. When Sam finished explaining what he had experienced, Lizzie said, "I have no clue what you are talking about as I have never experienced this myself, and I have no proof that what you say is true. But I can see that you are transformed by the experience and that you are joyful and passionate about it. I will learn from you how to experience this for myself."

So Sam showed Lizzie how to get enough momentum to push through the surface and see beyond it. Lizzie swam to the bottom of the pool, and then returned upwards at a fast pace. In her own way, Lizzie experienced exactly what Sam had experienced. When she returned, she said, "Now I know I was right to trust your enthusiastic passion. If I hadn't then I would never have known about this."

As you begin to trust that you are totally whole, do not need to read too much into the reactions of other people. Some people will be inspired by your newfound joy and energy. Most will remain uninterested.

STAYING AS GOD

YOU can witness your wholeness in a "peak state" or "spiritual experience". Certain experiences such as the exhilaration of winning a new job or the peace of meditation can provide windows into your wholeness. It is peak states and spiritual experiences that make God seem real and obvious. Even when these states and experiences end, you can still appreciate that your nature continues to be whole.

Imagine a friend came around to my house in the English countryside, and while we were drinking tea and chatting together, he suddenly jumped up out his chair and said, "I must get home to check my house still exists." I would think him rather odd and would enquire as to why he must do this. I would consider that since he has been in his house before, he knows it exists. The house does not rely on him being there so that it can exist. In the same way that your house exists whether or not you are actually in it, or even thinking about it, so too God exists within you even if you are not aware of it.

In my youth, I repeatedly went into experiences of "God awareness". I would experience my body expanding infinitely and my vision was flooded with white light. During these blissful experiences, I was convinced that God was my inherent nature. When these experiences faded, my self-limiting beliefs that I am only separate sometimes came back. After a little time of repeated experiences of wholeness I had to admit that I am God and always have been. Such a statement may sound like bragging or petulant, but I say it not to claim credit for myself. During these experiences it also became obvious that every person is also God, and that every living being is also God, and that every single atom in this fair universe is God. I saw that God was not only a creator but actually existed within every creation.

The opportunity to recognize God happens every day. When you witness any two parts of the world coming together to become one, then you are witnessing God. God is a raindrop falling into a puddle, it is two lovers kissing on a beach, or the mixing of ingredients together to make a cake. The opportunity to see God in the world is all around us. The exercise at the end of this chapter allows another opportunity to recognize God everywhere. Since you have always been God, there is nothing you have to do to *become* God. Recognizing God simply means accepting in your heart that you have always been God and always will be. The fruits of this are unimaginable. You will be able to step fully into your power, while knowing that you are no more or less powerful than any other.

Choosing to be more conscious of God can lead you to greater awareness of your nature. If you focus your attention on God then all experiences become spiritual. Watching TV, playing football, standing in the bus queue, filling out your tax return, and meditation, sex, music, and massage all become experiences of God. This is because it is *you* as God that is experiencing them.

Do the following exercise as much or as little as you wish, but at least once. It can open the door to God within you.

Exercise

Find somewhere comfortable where you won't be disturbed for a few minutes.

Sit in silence with your eyes closed for twenty minutes.

As you sit there, become aware of what is happening in your body and mind. Notice how your body feels, what emotions are there, and what you are thinking about.

Continue to be aware of physical sensations, feelings and thoughts.

Then relax a little and notice that these sensations, feelings and thoughts are in facts signals coming from your body and mind.

As you sit there, take your awareness to the one who is receiving these signals.

Notice that although you are experiencing these signals in your body and mind, the one who is experiencing them is not your body and mind.

Repeatedly take your awareness to the one that is receiving the signals.

QUESTIONS AND ANSWERS

Q: This is all great. I understand the principle of living as God to get benefits in my social, financial and working life but surely I can accomplish all these things without knowing that I am whole. I imagine many millionaires and famous artists get there because they lack a feeling of wholeness and this drives them on. Why then should I bother reconnecting with the sense of God I knew as a baby?

A: This is a good question. It is true that many people do not know themselves to be whole and therefore try to find it in the material world by amassing great wealth or fame. However, you must remember that their intention is not to get lots of money or become famous, but rather to get the feeling of wholeness that they hope will come with those accomplishments. However, invariably when they reach a certain level of financial or social success, they find they are empty of wholeness. This is because wholeness cannot be generated in outer experience. It is only when we become still enough to look inside that we can see that we have always been whole. Then we see we are God. The need to search for it in the outside world vanishes suddenly. Without a need to get a feeling of wholeness from the world, the world becomes a playground in which we are free to make money, become famous or do whatever we love. There is no longer an ulterior motive behind the acquisition of things. In other words, if you know you are God, then getting money will be for a financial reason, not for a existential one. You are therefore free from pressure and will be satisfied when you reach your goal. If goals are based on getting a sense of wholeness into your life, then they will be unsatisfying even after a success.

Q: Whenever I experience a sense of wholeness, it always disappears. For a split second, I experience God but then it goes. I return to earth with a bump and experience myself as being small and inadequate again. How can I make this experience stay?

A: Whenever you experience a glimpse of God in your life, you think to yourself that this is something bigger than you are. When you experience God, it is essential that you accept in your heart that you are God, and that for a moment you are experiencing that aspect of yourself. If I were to suggest that you experience the sensations in your right foot, you will probably put your attention there, even though you weren't aware of your foot before I mentioned it. Now when you forget about your foot, you will continue to act as if it is there. In other words, you will accept it is there without having to be aware of it. That acceptance isn't just mental knowledge. You don't have to say to yourself, "I know my foot is there because I have seen it, therefore I can use it to walk on." You simply know, "My foot is there and I don't need any proof of it." At some stage, you had an acceptance deep in your heart that your right foot is a rightful part of you. Similarly, in those moments of God awareness, you can accept that you are God. Then you will not rely on the recurrence of experiences to tell you that God is your nature.

Just as denying that the world is round doesn't change the shape of the world, denying that you are God doesn't change a thing. You are God whether you are aware of it or not. If you can suspend disbelief for just a few moments, then the next time you experience God you might notice how utterly familiar it is. It is so familiar because it is who you are!

PERSONAL STORY

ALEXANDER is a high-flying events organizer who found it very difficult to be in touch with "spirituality" during his fast-paced life. He decided to try the exercise I have described in this chapter to bring about a greater sense of calm and connectivity in his life. To begin with, he found it very difficult to still and silent. He said, "Every time I close my eyes, I have a huge amount of thoughts coming." Alexander saw this as a block to experiencing what lay behind the thoughts. I made a simple suggestion. I said to him "Who is having those thoughts?" He fell silent. Five minutes later he opened his eyes and smiled a big smile. "Now that I have realized that I am more than my thoughts, I can experience the whole of who I am." Alexander had experienced God - the part of him that receives and experiences all his thoughts.

2

Experience Uniqueness

"A wonderful realization will be the day you realize that you are unique in all the world. There is nothing that is an accident. You are a special combination for a purpose – and don't let them tell you otherwise... only you can fulfill that tiny space that is yours."
Leo Buscaglia

"There will always be dreams grander or humbler than your own, but there will never be a dream exactly like your own... For you are unique and more wondrous than you know!"
Linda Staten

"The unique personality which is the real life in me, I can not gain unless I search for the real life, the spiritual quality, in others. I am myself spiritually dead unless I reach out to the fine quality dormant in others. For it is only with the god enthroned in the innermost shrine of the other, that the god hidden in me, will consent to appear."
Felix Adler

"We have every reason to look forward into the future with hope and excitement. Fear nothing and no one. Work honestly. Be good, be happy. And remember that each of you is unique, your soul your own, irreplaceable, and individual in the miracle of your mortal frame."
Pearl S. Buck

WHO YOU ARE IS UNIQUE!

WHILE deep in the core of your being, you are one and the same as everyone else, on the surface you are obviously different. In fact, personally speaking, there is no one on earth like you! Your body, your mannerisms, your preferences, your actions and your thoughts all operate in a way that is different to those around you. This uniqueness is an expression of God moving through your life. Put simply:

Everyone is made from the very same God. However, your personal *expression* of God is totally unique.

You can make different actions, have different thoughts, look different, speak differently, move differently, love different things, and generally be very different from those around you. That you are distinct and unique is undeniable.

Why then, would you seek to be the same as everyone else? Why would a human being that is unique in all their glory hide in shame and strive to be similar to those around them? I have met people from all walks of life and the prevailing attitude is that truly alive people do not fit in to a system or structure. Whenever they try to, they feel that they are a square peg fitting into a round hole. People that are truly alive have to invent their own system to live within.

In the previous chapter, you got to see the beginnings of God awareness. That we are one with everything can be seen as a spiritual revelation or simply as our natural state. Either way, the recognition of your wholeness has an amazing effect on ordinary day-to-day life: you no longer need to feel whole by doing things the same as others. How many times in the past have you stifled your true expression to fit in to someone else's idea of what you should do or who you should be? This need not continue any longer. Since you are God the need to be whole by simulating wholeness can be relinquished. You can return to the natural innocence of being who you are.

A New Way of Being in the World

IMAGINE what it would be like if you got up in the morning and did exactly what you loved to do. I mean, what you really loved to do. Imagine what life would be like if you actually did whatever you loved to do, and you could do this every day. Take a moment to imagine. What would it look like? What would it feel like? What would you do? What would you be?

When I ask these questions to people at my workshops, they inevitably all come out with widely varying answers. "I would work with animals," says one woman. "I would spend more time with my son," says a man. "I would travel to Fiji" says another. "Play tennis", "Laugh more", "Start a new business", "Do charitable work", "Heal my back". One thing that is interesting is that when people show their true passions, they never have anything malicious or nasty to say. They want to reach into their hearts and cast a magic spell of improvement, joy and contribution.

What I find intriguing is that over time, people forget their dreams. They learn ways of behaving in the world that simply is not their true wish. They give up their ambitions and write off their passions as meaningless indulgence in a world that thrives on hard work, toil and struggle. It is true that survival does need to be taken care of, and that many of us need to work so we can be fed and sheltered. However, when you ask yourself if you are going about this in the way that you love most, what is the answer? If you imagined a scenario where the answer would continually be "yes", what would that be like?

The Richness of Experience

DURING life, it is the experience of events that give them meaning not the events themselves. If the England cricket team beats the Australians, the English fans would be very happy but the Australian ones would be miserable. They both experienced the same match very differently, and therefore had very different meanings for it.

When I was a young boy, I was with my family on the west coast of Ireland. During a sunny August day we went on a trip to a local beach, a lovely mile-long stretch of white sand. I was playing with my brother when my father told me he had found something in a cave nearby that I should see. I went into the dark cave with him, and he pointed to a curvy shape on the ground. As my eyes adjusted to the darkness, my father said in a scary voice, "It's a snake!" I became very scared and wanted to run from there but I stood my ground, partly out of bravery and partly because I was in shock. Then my father chuckled, and picked it up. We walked towards the light at the entrance of the cave and I could see that he was holding a piece of driftwood.

How you perceive events is how you make up reality. Since your experience of an event is what gives it meaning, it makes sense to invest your time, energy and your money in improving your experience of life. If you have a wondrous experience of something very simple, then you are richer than having a miserable experience of something very grand. I have met wealthy film stars with chips on both shoulders about what they had to do to get where they are. Conversely, I have met toilet attendants who are very grateful for their life. I bet you can guess who was enjoying life more. This is not to say that financial wealth is an obstacle to enjoyment. It isn't. What these people showed me was that it is your experience of what you have, what you do, and who you are that counts not the actual matter of what you have, what you do and who you are. If this sounds simple (which it is – I like to keep things very simple), then take a moment to consider how often this is neglected and ignored in day-to-day life on this planet. If our experience of events was honored as being more important than the events themselves, then having the "proper" lifestyle would be inconsequential. We could live any way we wished so long as the experience was one of joy and love.

GETTING INTO YOUR FLOW

YOU may be wondering what experience has to do with being unique. Well, if you imagined what it would be like to have that day where love prevailed and your ordinary constructs were given a new freedom, then you may have tasted the answer. After all, if you are to be alive on this planet, the most empowering question to ask yourself is not "Will I live?" but "How shall I live?" Since any adult who has a healthy mind and body is an expert in survival, the emphasis can shift from mere *surviving* to the joyous experience of *thriving*.

When you are know that you are inherently whole, God is allowed to flow into form. What God does when it flows into form is to create your human life, as well as all the other parts of the Universe. The acceptance of your nature as God means that this universal flow can be honored. This means that the way God makes your life is not tampered with or adulterated. You can let God form who you are without resistance. God flows through the heart and into life, and it is in the heart that the answers to who you really are can be found.

What is it that you love? The answer to this question defines your nature as a human being. It defines the things you wish to do, the people you wish to be with, the way you wish to do things and the places you wish to go in life. Any dishonoring of what you love is also a movement against the flow of God. To be in a job that you don't love is to dishonor the way God made you. To be in a relationship you don't love is the same. On the other hand, have you noticed how much "you" is being expressed when you are in a job or a relationship you love. Don't you feel like you are being yourself again and again and again? Doesn't that feel amazing?

To notice the aspects of your life that are truly unique, try the following exercise.

Exercise

Write down everything that you do in a day. For example, wake up, brush my teeth, eat breakfast, feed dog, etc. Write at least thirty things.

Go through each of these things and for each one write down how you do it. Use adjectives to describe how you carry them out. For example:
Reluctantly – lovingly – hungrily – hurriedly etc.

Now write down everything you would love to do in a day if you had no limitations of time, money or geography. For example, play tennis, dive in the Great Barrier Reef, eat a tasty nutritious meal, etc. Again, write at least thirty things.

Again, go through these events and describe how you would do them if you could. For example
Playfully – awesomely - satisfyingly.

Read through these preferences and characteristics. This is a map of what you do, how you do it, what you would love to do and how you would do it if you could.

Notice the differences between what you do and what you would love to do.

Notice the differences between how you do things and how you would do the things you love.

Finally, notice how the things you do, the things you would love to do, the way that you do these things, and the differences between them are about YOU. How many other people in the world would come up with exactly the same list as you have?

Questions and Answers

Q: Surely if I am God, then there is no difference between who I am and who another person is. How can I understand that I am God and yet unique at the same time?

A: There is a point at which spiritual understanding is not necessary and you have reached it. We do not need to understand this if we experience it. We do not need to understand how a rose can be beautiful if we experience it as such. If people say a rose is beautiful and we cannot experience that beauty then we may seek understanding of how it can be so. Deep down, as God, we are all one. On the surface, we each express spirit as a single human being (or a hedgehog, or a blade of grass, or a pencil…). Now, if you were to ask how we can be both a human being *and* God, then by your very asking you would exclude yourself from experiencing yourself to be both. Most people are good at experiencing their uniqueness, knowing their differences from those around them, sometimes even refusing to get involved with others that are too different. However, what most people have missed is that God is within them. Continue to do the exercise (from the first chapter) and let it guide you to an experience of God. Then the question evaporates. Knowing you are whole can mean that your uniqueness becomes very useful and is no longer a burden that blocks the experience of connectedness. When you no longer need to find God in the world, then you can be truly different in the world. You can be YOU.

Q: I went through a phase in my life a few years back where I felt totally peaceful with who I was, but more recently I have felt uncomfortable. Somewhere along the way I feel as though I have compromised my true self to be someone that I am not. How can I recapture that peace of being the true "me"?

A: Being true to yourself is an art that everyone can learn. There is a massive amount of pressure on us, especially when we are young, to conform. We are told to behave a certain way that suits the adults around us. So, we learn how to repress our natural love of things in order to be who other people want us to be. This habit can come back again later in life. We liberate ourselves from the confines of other people's expectations when we follow the heart. The way God flows in to form is through the heart. God in purity is completely formless, but when it flows through your heart it creates form: the form of your feelings, your thoughts, and your actions. The heart is a gateway between pure God and God in form. The easiest way for you to reconnect with your heart and therefore live authentically is to *do what you love*. When life is a succession of spontaneous loving acts, then your true nature is revealed. You get to enjoy the experience of 'being yourself' all day and every day.

Personal Story

Vanessa turned up at my office on the verge of tears. "I just don't seem to be able to do things in life the way I want to. I am a people pleaser, always have been and I'm afraid that I always will be," she told me. Vanessa had been married for fourteen years, had three children, and was divorced thirteen years ago. Since the children had grown up and left home, Vanessa finally had the time to look at how she wanted to live. It was at this stage that she realized she had been short-changing herself by placing herself at the bottom of a demanding heap, which included her mother, husband, children and boss. Vanessa was a classic example of this phrase:

If you don't define your path in life, someone else will.

If this happens, you will end up living your life for catering for other people's needs and forgetting how to look after yourself. This is what had happened to Vanessa. While there are times when we must put other people first, Vanessa had a habit of doing it all the time. She hoped she would gain approval and be loved by those she promoted to 'more important' than her. I asked Vanessa to do the exercise from this chapter and we discovered some interesting things. She had a hidden passion for painting that she had never manifested. She loved animals and yet never had pets because her mother used to tell her they were unhygienic. She was a keen piano-player and sorely wished to be playing in a band. We also discovered that although she appeared to be shy and retiring, she actually loved to do things in quite a raucous and celebratory way. With regular coaching, Vanessa changed her way of doing things to include more and more of what she loved. She implemented practical changes such as painting at home, joining a jazz band, and getting a cat. Over a space of about three months, she began to realize how unique and different from others she was. More importantly, she began to enjoy that fact.

3

EXPERIENCE THE WHOLE RANGE OF YOURSELF

"Be who you are and say what you feel because people who mind don't matter and people who matter don't mind."
Dr. Seuss

"What is important is to be present in this life, learn to transform stress into vitality, develop compassion through love, recycle energy to keep the body healthy and in harmony with mind and spirit, learn to understand true nature as spirit – then you are open to possibilities beyond the cycle of life and death."
Mantak Chia

"The privilege of a lifetime is being who you are."
Anonymous

"Thousands of candles can be lighted from a single candle, and the life of the candle will not be shortened. Happiness never decreases by being shared."
Buddha

God Recognition for Individual Empowerment

WHILE this is very reassuring, how does it relate to your daily life? If God is so warm and safe, why not stay in the experience of it always? The answer is that you simply cannot stay in any experience forever. Experiences change, sometimes through choice, sometimes through destiny.

I often tell my workshop participants the story of a man that escapes to a remote mountain cave in the Himalayas. He stays up on the mountain meditating, eating berries and forgetting his worries. For thirty years he sees no other human. He lives a simple life in deep spiritual solitude. He uses the peace of the forest around him to maintain a state that he believes is enlightenment. Indeed, this has been his experience for thirty years. Then, one day, an eight-year-old tourist wanders past the entrance to his cave playing a handheld Gameboy. As soon as he hears the sound of civilization, all his amazing states crumble. He screams at the boy for disturbing his peace and has to begin from scratch the process of regaining his inner balance.

There is no use in running into the spiritual existence as an escape from suffering individual life, for the individual life remains and will be re-experienced at some point. Likewise, there is no use in denying God by living an ignorant, egotistical, self-centered individual existence. Healing requires balance. We must accept the full range of our being *and* experience it in order to be healed.

To heal the divide between God and the material world, you must first recondition yourself from believing them to be separate to seeing them as one. If you have lived a predominantly outward looking, isolated, individualistic life, then you have to experience God to become balanced. Likewise, if you have lived a predominantly introspective, contemplative, holistic life then you have to get involved in the detailed interaction of individual life to become balanced.

To complete this healing process, we have to integrate the apparent opposites of God and matter. God needs grounding in matter.

Matter needs expansion in God. We need growth *and* security. We need to explore *and* to belong. We need to recognize our inherent nature as simultaneously being God *and* an individual.

One good way to accomplish this is to do work that spiritually nourishes us. By working from the heart, we can do activities in a way that is in accordance with the flow of God in our hearts. If we are comfortable with our material activities reflecting the flow of God, and vice versa, then we experience reconciliation between the two aspects. The open expanse of God can materialize in our lives as an opening and expanding of our belief systems (mental), our expression and communication (emotional), and our bodily agility and strength (physical).

It is worth mentioning that we don't have to restrict our individual lives through rules about diet, techniques, sexuality, media input or lifestyle in order to maintain our awareness of God. When we are assured of our awareness through repeated experience of it then we can let go of any methods that once led to that assurance. They are no longer essential for us to recognize that we are God. Likewise, we do not have to discard "spiritual techniques" as redundant now that we have recognized. For instance, yoga and meditation may become less useful to telling us that we are God but they can still remain very useful for cleansing the mind or relaxing the body.

When you become aware of God flowing into form, you can begin to manifest that which your heart desires. It is then that you realize your full potential as a human. When this becomes normal for you, then you will have a clarity out of which your life-purpose will be born. You can create your purpose according to what you love and where you are destined to go. When this happens, you will experience equality between activity and rest. Your experience of both will be deeper. The presence *or* absence of movement in your life will become a source of delight. With this, the stillness of God can meet face-to-face with the activity of personality to become equal partners in a dance of harmony. This dance heals the very split that once divided "person" and

"God". Instead of wanting the activity of personality or the resting of God, you can experience both instead. This is the key to wholeness.

Ultimately, like any healing, you must find your own way. This process is all about you being yourself in a way that you want, that you love, and that you fully enjoy. Following my guidelines or anyone else's can only be supportive in building confidence. You can find out what heals you. Then you can live as one whole human being: spiritual, individual and connected.

WHAT ARE YOU EXACTLY?

IMAGINE for a moment that you are a straw, like the one you would get with a milkshake. At each end of the straw are different aspects of yourself. At the top end of the straw is your individual nature. At the bottom end is God, your spiritual nature. Just as you can take your awareness right now to your left hand, your awareness can be anywhere on the straw. You can put your awareness to either end of the straw and experience yourself as being that. For example, you could take your awareness to the top of the straw and experience total individuality. You could also take your awareness to the bottom of the straw and experience yourself as the infinite love of God. Putting your awareness halfway up the straw would result in an experience of your "soul" that is individual to you but is also vast in nature like God is. Whatever you are aware of forms your experience of who you are. When awareness is at the top end of the straw, you would be forgiven for thinking that you were only a person and nothing else. Likewise if your awareness was at the bottom end (the goal for many spiritual traditions) then you might genuinely forget that you also exist as an individual person.

Most people live their lives at the individual end of the straw. Some reach the spiritual end, and a few try to stay there. You are in fact the whole straw. You are the whole range between the unity of God and the separate individuality of being human. While your experience of who you are changes, you actually remain the same.

Imagine now that you are that straw and that you are stuck into a ball of putty. Many other straws are also stuck into that putty ball. At the bottom end of the straw, you continue to experience God, sameness and infinity. At the top end, you continue to experience individuality, uniqueness and detail. When your experience moves to the bottom end, it is obvious to you that all the other straws also meet in the putty ball. It is obvious to you that, as God, all humans are essentially the same. Most struggles in life are ended by seeing the essential oneness of everything.

In order to feel that you belong in the universe, it is imperative to recognize that you are God. If you were to live life only at the individual end, you would look across to all the other tops of the straws and be convinced that everyone was separate. You would see many other isolated individuals. You may try to gain connection with them, but this is difficult unless you first make that connection at the God end. You would have to bend your straw to get closer to the top of another, and this means a whole lot of effort. It may also be a direction that you do not wish to go, and are only doing because of a lack of inner connectedness.

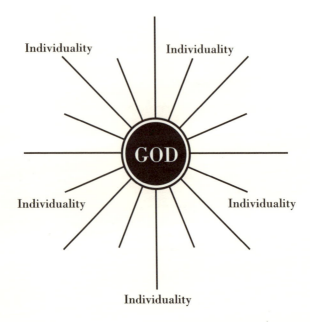

We are, of course, all inherently deeply connected. The difference between us is who recognizes this fact and who ignores it. If you have lived most of your life experiencing the individual end of the straw, then you may have missed the experience of deep inner connectedness that lies at the God end. Once you gain some balance of experience by recognizing God as your essential nature then you can begin to appreciate that you are the entire straw. You will notice that you are not only the part of it that you are currently experiencing. This means that even when you are deeply immersed in an individual experience, you can recognize that you are unified with everything else in the universe. Conversely, you can also recognize your unique expression and identity when immersed in experiences of total oneness. To live the entire range of your being is the key to being yourself, feeling comfortable, and thriving in this existence. This is the achievement of true balance in your life.

Achieving Balance

WHERE the middle way is, balance is. You can be a meditative spirit being *and* a self-sustaining person. The two are not exclusive to each other. If you become too inner-focused you can end up relying on others to support your outer existence. Although you might pray every day, you do not work to buy food. Likewise, if you become too externally focused you may lose your awareness of God. Although you may work nine to five every day to sustain your personal existence, you forget about the sacred space inside of you. The middle way allows you to combine both elements so that you can be an authentic, living, breathing, money-earning, spirit-embodying, creative, fun-loving person. You are both God *and* a person. To live both fully is to let God manifest in form without restriction. This is ultimately satisfying. This is authenticity.

Balance is lost is when you involve yourself too much in either the internal God realm or the external material world. These two places only exist as two separate places when you are out of balance. When you are in balance, they are one and the same. Commonly, the emphasis is to be overly involved in the external world. This is usually because there is *pain* in the internal realm that has not been faced. If you carry the burden of stored-up pain around with you then it acts to obstruct your connection with God. You can shy away from pain by getting heavily involved in external distractions like food, sex, drugs, relationships or TV. However being in touch with that pain is essential to completing the marriage of the internal and external realms. God flows no matter what obstructions you put in the way. The blocks of pain that you put in the way of God's flow may have been stored up since babyhood. It is therefore *essential* that you reconnect with that pain and release it in order that you may grow into the harmony of balance. When that pain is felt, it is released and the flow of God through the heart becomes broader. As more and more pain is felt and let go of, the heart grows ever more courageous and in its expansion allows more and more of God to filter *directly* into your personal life. This God energy is your *infinite potential*. When it flows freely into your personal life you can use it to achieve your goals, as we shall see later in the book. This is because whatever you do will be carrying with it the current of destiny. God flowing into your personal life means that destiny is supporting your personal choices and your personal choices are congruous with destiny. What you love to achieve will happen.

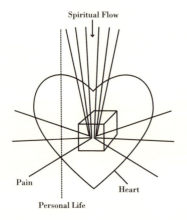

1. Pain randomly distributes spiritual flow, allowing only some to get into your personal life.

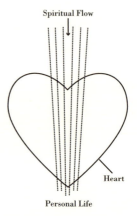

2. Pain is released allowing spiritual flow to empower personal life.

To feel the obstructions of pain is essential to opening up your spiritual flow to personal life. This is why so many mystics talk of the "dark night of the soul". Sometimes, we need to be alone (*very* alone) in order to feel this old pain. No one can hold your hand in such a space. It is the purging of a thousand tears, and yet it is joyous because life is enriched through it.

One of the ironies of recognizing your inherent wholeness is that in doing so you must acknowledge and accept all your past isolation. When such isolation is a day-to-day experience it is tolerable. However, when the recognition of God rears its magical head, then you must face the music of years of pretended isolation. Then you can leave that pain behind and enjoy the new life that lies ahead of you. It will be beyond your imagination.

CONTENTMENT AND PERSONAL GROWTH

ASK yourself: Do you want to be who you are? Do you want to be what you are being right now? In the future, do you want to continue being what you are being right now?

Whatever you make of these questions, remember this: you cannot help being authentic. Inside of you is a voice that knows the true "you". When you let that voice talk for you, you will honor your authenticity. If you choose to do so that then you will slowly give up any pretences. You will speak from your innermost, you will do what you love, and you will flow with the universe. However, if you choose to dishonor your authenticity you will battle against seemingly artificial situations. You will not be able to say what you want to, you will do things out of guilt or duty, and you will feel that you really don't fit in the world. Contentment stems from honoring your own authenticity.

Personal growth is the movement out of dishonor, and into honor, of your own authenticity. The moment you decide to allow your personal life to come under the guidance of God is the moment you have started to grow towards authenticity. An authentic person accurately reflects the God that they are. They feel that they fit into the universe. This is how flowers live, and trees and porcupines, even carrots, and parrots, and ... you get the idea ...

You can most easily change from dishonor to honor when you let go of trying to change others. All the energy that goes into trying to control others and trying to bring them into honor of their authenticity is actually a sign of inner despair. It means that you have not yet opened out enough to fully face your own demons. Instead, you can safely concentrate on the demons of others. It is the perfect distraction: "Oh no, I don't like the look of this inside of me, but don't think about that–look at that other person instead, how terrible, tut-tut ... ".

Controlling others by guiding them into authenticity can be a substitute for your own inability to do so. When you cease to do that then you can stop misplacing your energies and concentrate on yourself. You simply can't improve yourself by improving other people. The temptation is obvious: there is minimal risk involved in improving someone else. However if you were to improve yourself, you would lose much (negative habits, for example). And loss can be painful, even losing something you don't particularly like. It is the stress of adaptation. You must learn to 'fit into' your new personality as you become more authentic. It may even feel artificial to begin with. Living as an authentic person will reconnect you with the whole cycle of life. You may feel that it is very new and very familiar at the same time.

The Circle of Authenticity

AS babies, we are authentic. Most of us lose our authenticity through fear, pain and unexpressed emotion. We learn to survive and in doing so we sacrifice our integrity and lose our sense of wholeness. To reclaim this state in life means closing the opened loop of the past.

We can become authentic like a baby *and* powerful like an adult. But this can only happen when we cease controlling others and begin to use that energy to let go of our own pretence. For it is that pretence that stops us enjoying the vibrant richness that is an authentic life.

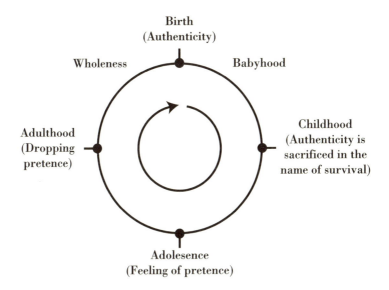

Getting Confident

THERE is one major block to being totally authentic: lack of confidence. Sometimes, all you need is to be told by someone that it is okay to be who you are and do what your heart desires. Sometimes this is enough to propel you into becoming a personal manifestation of God. This is education. This is the passing on of knowledge that "you can". If you ever find yourself in a situation where you long to be authentic, simply tell yourself, "I can." As you grow in confidence, so your ability to be authentic grows. You can be who you are without apology. Such great acknowledgement of your own self-worth leads to greater respect and trust in yourself, which in turn encourages respect and trust from others.

When you are rooted in your personality as being a direct expression of God, then you experience security and stability. Security and stability are essential in order to have sustainable contentment.

Temporary contentment is easy to come by. Lasting contentment comes only when we tread the middle path between God and personality, between spirit and matter. When we tread the middle path, the two opposites on either side of us become balanced, and cease to pull us away from authenticity. It is then that we can be who we are without struggle. Then you awaken to the nature of this life:

>Spirit is matter, matter is spirit, God is you, you are God, and inner and outer are one. *This is balance.*

Authenticity is Satisfying

BEING authentically yourself is the only road to satisfaction. If *you* do not satisfy yourself, then you will never be satisfied. How can you satisfy yourself unless you know who you are? If you do not know who you are, then who will you satisfy? Someone else? The "you" that you believe you are? You must know who you are if you are to satisfy yourself.

Authenticity can be reached through three steps:
1. Recognizing yourself as God.
2. Finding out who you are as an individual.
3. Manifesting your desires.

The first step uncovers the big picture. It reveals you to be a being of love. The second step is the detailed picture. This is where you discover everything about yourself as an individual in the newfound light of spiritual recognition. You find out what you really want, what you like, what you prefer, and what will satisfy you. This step must come second, because discovering yourself as an individual without first recognizing yourself as God will lead to a distorted judgment as to what your needs really are. The third step is the action that brings God and individuality together. It is a harmonious manifestation of your desires, wants, preferences and likes in your life. This is essential for wholeness and integration. Action that is congruent with both your spiritual and individual aspects will close the gap between those two sides of yourself.

At its peak, all action becomes an expression of God in the world. Work, play and relationships become a full, vibrant, outstanding flow of passionate energy. Such a flow cannot be obstructed by fear. Fear is what appears to keep your spiritual and individual aspects separate. Courage is what rejoins them. And since the heart is the root of all courage, it is the heart that is the grounding point between God and the individual.

It is entirely possibly to experience the whole range of yourself. It simply means that you are willing to experience your self as God, and to see that God flows in all things. If this experience is accepted as "real" then knowing your infinite nature when you are focused on a worldly task will be easy. The following exercise assists with this subtle balancing act by training you to become more able to relate to experiences of God when you are involved in everyday activity:

Exercise

Spend a few minutes centering yourself by sitting quietly.

Allow any thoughts, feelings or physical sensations to come and go.

If you feel a connection to God within yourself, then become accustomed to what it is like, what brought it about, and how you feel about it. For example, it may be when you thought of a sunny beach or it might be a feeling of lightness accompanied by white light.

Now get up and do some gentle activity like stretching your body or washing your face.

As you this gentle activity, keep in your awareness the factors that were surrounding that connection to God.

For example you can continue to think of a sunny beach, or notice any lightness in your body and any white light around you.

Notice how much of the inner experience is mirrored back to you by things around you in the outer world.

Again, sit quietly and centre yourself.

When you connect with God use your senses to become accustomed to the features and qualities of the experience.

Next, try a slightly more vigorous activity like taking a walk, or washing the dishes.

Again, connect the God experience to the action by noticing any similarities.

Do this twice more, sitting and moving, each time doing a more involving activity.

Questions and Answers

Q: I find I am in a very peaceful space when I sit down and relax quietly. However, whenever I get involved in work or relationships, I get very anxious and often cannot bear to face the world. What is going on and why can I not seem to be relaxed when I am being active?

A: When we sit quietly, we can become at ease with what is around us. We can contact God within ourselves and are in a kind of calmness because we know who we truly are. If this state of calmness disappears in activity it is because we are no longer aware that we are connected to God. It is as if the activity can take us out of that peaceful space. The key to remaining in a state of peace continually is to be aware of God while in the midst of activity. This inner awareness can be held even when we are focused outside of ourselves. It is an art that can be learnt, just as any art can be. If you are in the activity of work or relationships then an extreme thought, emotion, or physical sensation, can grab your attention. When this happens, it can seem like you are out of touch with God. You become so concentrated on the world of separation that you forget who you really are. You can take your awareness back to God by transcending the situation. This means that you widen your perspective using any means possible. This can be as simple as breathing more deeply, or closing your eyes momentarily to reconnect with the God that you are. You can find a reliable way of reminding yourself that you are God by noticing what is happening to you when you are in peak states of God recognition. For example, you may be singing a song when you find yourself aware of God. You can repeat the words of that song in your head to remind you of your nature as God. This is similar to a religious ritual except that *you* have devised it to be the most effective method for *you*.

Q: I feel most balanced when I am around other people. It is like I forget my worries and lose myself in them. I feel confident and happy. When I am alone I don't feel so good. How can I hold onto those great feelings of confidence and happiness when I am alone?

A: Human relationships can be a great source of God recognition and in a social space you can see more clearly your nature as God. However, when you are alone you drift back into a state of individuality and this can be disturbing and upsetting. Only when you cease to move backwards and forwards between the perception that you are God and the perception that you are an individual will balance be found. Notice I say "perception". This is because you are God *and* an individual. If you believe yourself to be only one or the other, this is only a perception. It is the perception that you are only one part of yourself. When you are able to accept that you are God even when you are experiencing your individuality, then you will be free of needing to hold on to God. We cannot keep God. We cannot keep what we always are. Why not? Because we are it always and cannot lose it, therefore keeping it is impossible.

Personal Story

MARTIN had been a very wealthy legal professional and had walked out on his job at the age of forty-one and left Europe to travel the world. He became aware of God at this time, or as he called it "the Higher Self". He saw this as a higher power that had to be worshipped. When he returned to Europe after four years of traveling, he found it very hard to fit in again. He knew he wanted to be part of a stable community and live in his homeland. However, he was very sensitive to the cutthroat business activities of the western world. He found that it distracted him from his worship of his "Higher Self". After talking with Martin for half an hour it became evident that upon discovering God, he had disconnected with it in order to create a rational explanation for what had happened to him. He said, "I couldn't take on board that I was that vast. To be infinite seemed too scary for me." He tried to put it outside himself as a higher part of him that he could then relate to. This ended up with him becoming very disturbed by activity around him. After all, if you are having a relationship with something, then that relationship can be disturbed by environmental activity. However, if you have always been that, then no amount of environmental activity can take you away from it. For example, you would never forget your name no matter how busy you were. It is guaranteed one hundred per cent! We worked with Martin's acceptance of being his "Higher Self", which at first seemed difficult but after a few sessions he responded very positively saying, "For the first time I feel comfortable knowing that I am as vast as the entire universe". If this sounds a little odd, then consider what happened in his life next: he stayed in Europe, got a job which he loved very dearly, he met a woman and married her two years later. He now lives with his new family and loves his life, which is very active and very rooted in God recognition.

PART 2

KNOW YOURSELF

Experiencing yourself to be everything from God to an individual human being and everything between provides the fuel for empowering actions. But to light that fuel, you have to know where, when and how to make these actions. This requires a greater awareness about your personal nature. This part of the book is dedicated to looking at ways of becoming more aware of who you are and how you can best let that flow in the world.

4

KNOW WHEN TO ACCEPT AND WHEN TO ACT

"God grant me the Serenity to accept the things I can not change,
the Courage to change the things I can,
and the Wisdom to know the difference."
Fourteenth-century Prayer

"It is the metaphysically given that must be accepted: it cannot be changed. It is the man-made that must never be accepted uncritically: it must be judged, then accepted or rejected and changed when necessary."
Ayn Rand

"If you haven't the strength to impose your own terms upon life, you must accept the terms it offers you."
T.S. Eliot

"Vision without action is a daydream. Action without vision is a nightmare."
Japanese Proverb

The Cards of Life

IN my teens, I played the card game of bridge at international level. Through playing cards, I came to learn that the first principle of successful card playing was to accept the cards you have and work with them. If I had been dealt a poor hand I noticed that I could find hidden jewels within the cards and make a play that I would have otherwise missed had I not been so keen to make the best of them. I noticed that the more and more I concentrated on working with what I had, and the less and less I concentrated on what might have been, the more likely I was to play successfully and win games.

It is said that of all card games, bridge is the one that requires the most skill, having a skill factor of 50 per cent and a luck factor of 50 per cent. The skill factor represents self-empowered choices. It was my freewill to determine events based upon my action. The luck factor represents destiny. It is the uncontrollable chance of drawing certain cards or having the luck of the play. The good news in bridge is that you can increase your chances of success by applying skilful freewill. You don't rely solely on the cards you were dealt.

It is the same in life. We are all dealt different cards in life, yet we still have the potential to make the most of our cards should we desire to do so. While we may be dealt a poor hand, we can vastly increase our chances of success by accepting it and playing it skillfully. At the same, if we are dealt a good hand, we can guard against the belief that destiny has done all the work by continuing the motivation to play well.

I always feel that a poor hand played well is much better than a good hand played lazily. We have no control over the initial deal we get in life, e.g. our parents, our race, our financial status, our geographical location, our religion, etc. We are dealt these as babies. As we go through life playing our cards, we get to choose whether we want to be successful or not. Do you want deep, intimate relationships? Do you want an empowering career? Do you want a loving family? Do you want financial flexibility? Do you want to honor yourself? Do you want to be honest? Do you want to be valued and appreciated? Do you want to enjoy yourself?

While 50 per cent of the answers to these questions will be laid out by destiny, the other 50 per cent are up to you. If you choose success in your life, and work to make it happen, then it will come. It is as simple as making a choice and then following through on it with commitment.

If you do not exercise choice in your life, then your cards will be played randomly and they are less likely to fall in your favor. If you do not exercise the massive power of choice you hold at every moment of your life, then you sacrifice your freewill. When you give it up, the freewill aspect of the game is controlled by other players. To be fully yourself in the world, you have to exercise your power of choice. To know more about when to exercise your power of choice, it is useful to know what is possible to predict and what is impossible.

WHAT WE CAN PREDICT AND WHAT WE CANNOT

SOME things can be predicted. When we become aware of destiny playing itself out around us, accurate predictions become much simpler. Destiny can be illustrated using the leisurely environment of a billiard table. If you were to hit a ball, it would move and bounce off the other balls and cushions until it comes to rest. If you knew enough about the dynamics of the table, the smoothness of the felt, the elasticity of the cushions, and so forth, then you can make a fairly accurate prediction about where the ball will end up. However, predictions can always be undermined. For example, a zebra falling through the roof and landing on the billiard table would not only surprise you but also radically change where the ball ends up.

The law of destiny says that something only happens because something else preceded it. For example, a ball only moves on the table because it was hit by another ball that was struck by a cue. The law of destiny also says that the zebra only fell through the roof because of an event that preceded it, for example, a person pushing it out of an airplane.

The point is that you reliably predict events in life if you have enough local information about the environment in which it is happening. We tune in to destiny by perceiving what is possible and making an action. When we strike a billiard ball, we are predicting what will happen to it based on what we know about the table and the environment. Since we know nothing about a parachuting zebra, we cannot predict that it will fall through the roof.

A sequence of events could be reliably predicted if all information about all possibilities is available. Trying to know all this information in your mind is a struggle, but there is a way you can do it that takes far less effort and yields far greater rewards:

You can *tune in* to destiny and feel it in your body.

This tuning in is commonly called intuition, gut instinct, psychic ability or predictive ability. It is basically a prediction based on a physical sensation in the body. It leaves you knowing what will happen next without needing a mental explanation to back up that prediction. Trusting these intuitive predictions can be of great benefit in your empowering journey through life. Doing so frees life up from being a struggle.

KNOWING THE DIFFERENCE BETWEEN DESTINY AND FREEWILL

LIFE becomes a struggle in two ways: either we fight to make something happen that is destined not to happen, or we fail to exercise our willpower when there is something we absolutely can change. To avoid struggling in either of these two ways, we have to know what is destined and what is within the range of our willpower.

An obvious example of destiny is the sun setting. We have no control over it, and it is going to set whether we enjoy that fact or whether we fight against it. It is simply bigger than our personal power so to enjoy it fully and to avoid struggle we must *accept* that it is destined to set.

Freewill is very different. Imagine you get up in the morning and you choose which clothes you are going to wear. This choice is obviously something within your control, so freewill determines what color clothes you choose and what combination you wear that day.

As we shall see later on, destiny and freewill while seeming to be very separate are actually indistinguishable in a balanced life. In other words, when we become balanced, we use our willpower to achieve what is destined to happen anyway, and what is destined to happen is what we would will to happen if we could.

The intention of this book is to bring balance into your life. As we proceed, you should be able to notice tangible changes in the way you view destiny and freewill. This new view can empower you to greater ease and comfort in day-to-day life.

As I traveled around the world, I met a number of interesting people. Among them were fundamentalists whose beliefs strongly stated that everything in life was destined. When someone came to them with a condition such as depression, for example, they would be tell them that destiny had made them depressed. The person would go away feeling that nothing could be done and that they would have to stay depressed. This view may have been useful for some retired people and social drop-outs, who found that no longer having to be responsible for anything was a relief. However, it seemed unbalanced to me. Having worked with people claiming to be depressed and seeing that state being changed very quickly, I know that you *can* make a difference to the state you are experiencing. Belief in destiny is popular because believers do not need to take life too seriously if they are simply characters in a play. Nor do they have to be burdened with the unnecessary responsibility of guilt. However, there is a danger in believing in destiny alone: it can promote apathy and quitting. After all, if your life story is totally written for you, then what motivation do you have to participate in it or to better it? If depression was "destined" then why not let it continue for the rest of your life? If your life is "destined" to be miserable and uncomfortable, then where is the motivation to change it? Beliefs that are balanced reap the greatest fruits.

Other people I met claimed that everything was within our control, and that anything was possible. Again, I found this to be unbalanced since I had never seen these people eat a planet or fly across the solar system. It seemed to me that some things were beyond mere human control. While often an empowering way to see the world, some people that dogmatically followed this belief seemed to be frustrated by a never-ending stream of unfinished goals and aspirations.

Since these ideas were not "truth" and simply a way of perceiving the world, I asked myself, "What way of perceiving the world would give the greatest enjoyment, power, and passion to my life?" It seemed obvious that both camps of people had validity in their beliefs. Some things are definitely within our control, while other things definitely are not. The things that are out of our control are matters of great size like our nature as God. Things that we can control are matters of detail like our nature as a person.

On an individual level, life is made up purely of choice. Personal choice is a kind of magic. To learn this magic, you must learn the tools that empower you to choose. The less you have this power, the more the important choices in your life will be made by others (for example, your partner, your parents, or your peer group). As God, you have no choice and destiny works its magic. Most life experiences occur somewhere in between and therefore encompass a measure of both personal choice and destiny.

Imagine, for a moment, the man in the office whose project has gone terribly wrong. He fights to make it work, worried of what will happen to his livelihood if he does not. When he realizes that he is not fully responsible for it not working, he can relax and let nature take its course. He can follow the problem to its root and work with the way it is, rather than fighting against it. This may mean having to drop the project altogether, often times revealing a more powerful path. Or it may mean adapting the project to work with forces beyond his control. This is where knowing the difference between what is destined and what is controllable becomes useful day-to-day stuff. For example, imagine an insomniac who believes that there is nothing they can do about their sleep. They simply believe that it is destiny playing a cruel trick on them. They do nothing to alleviate their condition and they tolerate a situation that can easily be changed. Knowing that they can control their quality of sleep can be the key to them finding out what they need to do. They may search for therapies or techniques to assist in better sleep, eventually coming across something that works for them.

You cannot change destiny (for example, when the sun sets) but you can change your individual response to destiny (for example, whether you look at the sunset or not). To know the boundaries between individual choice and destiny is to have clarity. This clarity shows you when to use your power to make a choice and when to surrender to the inevitable. If you are confused about the boundary between choice and destiny, then you may struggle. The struggle of trying to change something that is destined is enormous. Likewise, to give up on something that only you are responsible for is a tragedy.

Finding the boundary between choice and destiny is essential to living a life full of power. This is the power to be *yourself*. Where there is a balance between choice and destiny, between will and surrender, between action and rest, then there is the power to be yourself.

Theories, philosophies and beliefs are common and varied. We can get them off the shelf from anyone and add them to our perceptual shopping basket. Just like food, these theories, philosophies and beliefs are not important in terms of what they are, but in terms of how they affect our lives. It is not what we believe that matters but how that belief affects our experience of existence.

KNOWING THE DIFFERENCE

THE benefits of knowing when you can change a situation and when you cannot are great. The question is, how do you learn to know when to act and when to accept?

Well, there are some easy steps to take to assist in this. First, you have to start doing things from your heart. This means that what you love takes precedence over all other actions in your life. What you love comes before what you fear or what you feel you ought to do. When you make this subtle but life-affirming shift, you will begin to see the difference between freewill and destiny and how the two can be aligned to produce balance in your life. When you act from your heart, you will find yourself moving towards things that really matter to you, things that you love. If you can have the things that you love, then there is no problem. If you cannot, then knowing whether you can change the situation or not will make life unimaginably easier.

You can tell whether you are able to instigate change in a situation by trying to make a change that you would love to see. If this change happens, then it is within the realm of freewill and next time around you can remember that. However, if change does not come easily and naturally, then you have to drop the way you were trying to make changes and try something new. This might appear obvious but I have seen intelligent people going around in a continual circle trying unsuccessfully to remedy something over and over in the same way. If only they could step back. They would see that changing their strategy would increase their chance of making the change they want. Having this ability to change perspective from the smaller picture to the bigger picture is something we will encounter again and again in this book. It is powerful because if you can step out of the details and observe your life from the perspective of God then you can make changes to life much more easily.

From the space of God, life is a tiny expression within a vast whole, and can therefore be altered without much effort or risk. When you are focused on the details of life too much, then you can get caught in the perception that changing your life means changing your whole universe, because this is what it seems to be. If this is the case then changing your life will be both risky and laborious due to the colossal size of the undertaking.

So, to summarize the first two steps:
- Act from the heart.
- Drop strategies that do not work.

If you love something and you move toward it and can't reach it, then you can use different strategies. If you still cannot reach it, there will be a point when in your heart you recognize that you will never have it. This is the point at which you see it as destiny. Remember, though, that this is recognition in the heart. It is different to the mental concept of "I can't have this because I am not worthy." These kind of ideas should never be acted upon or given any power.

Over time, you will find that when you get involved in life and try out new things and new experiences, you will build up a huge reference bank to which you can refer. This means that you will be able to instantly identify what is destiny and what is freewill without having to go through the whole exercise of trying to change things to find out if it is possible or not. This means you develop a "feel" for destiny and a "feel" for freewill.

THE BALANCE OF DESTINY AND FREE WILL

DESTINY and free will go hand-in-hand. Destiny marks out the bigger picture while free will makes up the details. When the free will of individual action aligns with the direction of destiny, then we experience harmony in our reality. At these times, it seems as though everything is just the way it ought to be. Every action seems to fit a situation just like a foot would fit a shoe. This "fit" is the source of massive amounts of enjoyment in life. It is a deep belonging and a feeling of being connected to our environment.

Achieving a balance of destiny and free will in life takes awareness. When we can clearly distinguish those aspects of our lives that are in destiny's hand and those aspects that we have full choice over, then we can surrender to destiny while empowering ourselves to take responsible action. This balance gives us the best of both worlds. No longer do we struggle to control elements that we simply cannot control. Likewise, we do not give up on those elements that we can control. To give up controlling something that is within the sphere of our freewill is to give away our individual power, often straight into the hands of another person. When we choose to change aspects of our lives that are within our control then we take *responsibility* for our lives. We assume the mantle of our lives and we direct the flow of it.

When we are responsible for our lives, we have the power to choose *in all aspects where choice is possible*. We can choose our lifestyle, our diet, our dress sense, our career, our income, our place of residence and our reaction to circumstances. This self-empowerment does not overlook destiny. Rather it rides alongside it, for the more aligned our individual choices are with destiny, then the more powerful and successful they will be.

The dynamic of destiny can be read in the heart. The dynamic of freewill can be read in the gut. The gut is the steering wheel for individual direction. The heart is the engine. It is the motivational force of destiny propelling us forward.

Destiny and freewill stand beside each other in human life. To accept the interplay of both is to live a whole life that is fully surrendered to destiny and fully motivated for freewill. This is balance. To ignore one aspect results in you becoming either a quitter ("Everything is destined so I might as well give up".) or a control freak ("I can do whatever I want and it will always turn out the way I want it".)

When your will is aligned with destiny, you experience a distinct harmony. You appear to be in the right place at the right time. Everything seems to fit perfectly and appropriately. There is a strong sense of belonging. You are passionate about what you are doing. There is a sense of certainty that you are doing the right thing in the right way.

This alignment of will with destiny means that you are flowing the same on an individual level as you are on a spiritual level. This match in flow integrates your individual aspect with your spiritual aspect, making the difference between them *impossible to experience.*

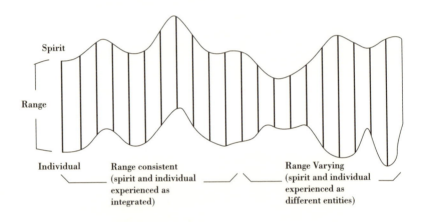

If we used the metaphor of surfing to illustrate this point, you could imagine that the sea represents destiny, and surfboard represents freewill. If you to were to do some surfing, the way you ride the waves depends on your use of the surfboard. In other words, the way you ride on the wave of destiny depends on how you use your freewill to steer through it. If you are in harmony with destiny, you will ride it successfully. However, if your will is in conflict with destiny, then you will crash.

To get anywhere, you need both the wave and the board. Imagine trying to surf by simply standing on your board on the beach. You would get some funny looks! Without the waves of destiny, the flow of the universe is not present, and no amount of freewill can move you anywhere. Now imagine trying to surf in the waves without a board. You get sucked under and thrown around with any control. You would have lost the tools of freewill that are necessary to navigate destiny.

When you successfully ride the waves of destiny, then you exercise freewill in a way that is *aware* of the forces of destiny. When you ride the wave with ease and ability, the whole world seems to conspire to assist and support you. As surfers would say, you are "in the zone". Your mind and body are in total harmony with God as you enter a state of free flow.

The experience of being in the zone is a feeling or experience filled with total joy, confidence, and trust. You may reach such states by making love, winning money, getting a job offer, scoring in football, or laughing at a movie. Being in the zone is a heightened experience of intimacy. Intimacy with God, with your mind, with your body, and with other people comes naturally. The question of how to achieve intimacy becomes meaningless for you are experiencing it first hand. It is easy to read any situation and flow with it. You can act as if you know what will happen next while at the same time assuming nothng at all.

When all your actions are in harmony with destiny, then the difference between freewill and destiny vanishes. This manifests as an experience of "becoming one with the universe". You strongly belong. You exist on all levels simultaneously. You are in balance. Your actions are destiny's actions and vice versa. The perceived difference between free will and destiny only exists when there is an imbalance between the two. If one is more dominant than the other in your life, then you will see a difference between them.

If you make life choices from your heart, then you will find an increase in the alignment between destiny and freewill. Life will open up to the harmonic flow of "coincidences" that exists at all times. Making life choices based on what you love, tunes you in to that flow. The coincidences are often bizarre and surprising. However, they will become less and less surprising to you as you get more and more used to them.

So, go forth and let your freewill flow from your heart in the form of active, self-empowered choices. This will increase success in your life. And remember, personal development is a game. Remember to enjoy it as you play.

EXERCISE

Write a list of ten things you would love to have, be or experience in your life that isn't already there.

Go through the list. For each of the ten things, work out how many different ways you have tried to reach each one. Write each different way down (some may have no ways at all, while others may have several).

Now write down new ways you can reach those things. Write at least three ways you could go about reaching each thing differently.

Take action by doing at least one new way of doing each thing.

As you do so, notice what your heart says about what you are doing. Get a sense whether doing the new way will get that thing or not. If you sense that it will not, then it is a sign that no amount of willpower will help and that you are destined not to reach it. However, if you get a sense that the new way of doing it will result in that thing being achieved then it is a sign that personal willpower can be used to get what is destined.

Questions and Answers

Q: I am happy when things go well in my life but as soon as things go pear-shaped, I crumble. Often times, I get ill at the slightest slip-up. At other times, I get overly anxious about something not working perfectly. How can I better enjoy my life without these kinds of struggle?

A: As soon as you identify those things you can control and those things that are out of control, you can cease to take responsibility for those things you cannot control and you can therefore take full responsibility for those things you can. I see so many people trying to take on a burden of responsibility that is way more than they need to. The result is that they get exhausted trying to do the things done that they have no power over. Over time, they actually start to get less and less responsible towards the things they can change. When you know what is outside of your control, you can let go of being responsible for it. With that, a whole lot of worry goes with it. You can begin to relax right now about things outside of your control and use you power and resources to work on what you can control. Also, remember that even when you can control something, you will not always make the best choice. Perfection is merely an idea. We learn by being "imperfect" and by finding out better ways to do things by being unafraid to fail. All successful people are able to face failure without getting ill or overly anxious about it. So, go into action knowing that it is impossible for everything to work out just the way you want it, even if it is in your control. This kind of acceptance, along with the acceptance of those things you cannot change will serve you very well.

Q: I believe that I can do anything if I apply enough willpower. Why should I even bother about destiny if this is the case?

A: Firstly, you cannot do anything simply by willpower. Imagine teleporting yourself to the North Pole right now. Or, imagine keeping an intelligent woman interested in you simply using willpower. Some things are simply not within your capability. However, the belief that you can do anything can be very useful to your performance in life *so long as it is not taken as the whole truth*. A runner who has very little chance in a race can improve their performance by believing they can win it. They may come further up the field with a belief like that. But if they use that belief to belittle themselves when it doesn't happen, it is worthless. The point of recognizing destiny is that you can surrender to forces greater than a human being. There are many times when do so makes life more enjoyable and comfortable. There are times in everyone's life where you simply cannot do what you would like. Successful people tend to see this as being circumstantial rather than a failure of their own power to get things done. If you start to see destiny as a force to be respected and worked within, it does not have to limit your power.

Personal Story

DAVID came to me absolutely bereft of ideas on how to change his working life. He felt as though whatever he tried, he could not work out what he was meant to be doing with his career. Having moved through numerous jobs, including a tennis coach, bank clerk, and a plumber, he was still scratching his head as to what his true vocation was. When I asked him what he loved to do, this came easily to him. His eyes lit up and he said he would love to be artistic but had never had the confidence to do so. This seems to happen with nearly everyone I meet – no matter how confused a person is, they always know deep down what it is that they love. Anyway, David was sure that he wanted to be a painter. In fact he said that it felt like his destiny. As usual, his heart knew his destiny. What he truly loved and what was destined for him were one and the same. After a lengthy discussion about his practical options, David decided that he was going to change his profession once again. One year later he returned to me saying that he had tried everything he could to make a living as a painter but nothing had worked. We looked at his strategies and in doing so realized that he hadn't actually tried everything. He went away again feeling very unsure whether painting was destined for him or whether he just believed that. After trying some of the new strategies we had devised, he had a successful exhibition and sold over fifteen paintings. He became joyous in his work. Three years on, he still works as a professional painter and loves it dearly. He knows it is his destiny and is glad he did not turn his back on it when it looked like he had tried everything. In his heart, he had never lost faith that painting was his true vocation.

5

Know What is Important to You

"A man who dares to waste one hour of life has not discovered the value of life."
Charles Darwin

"As human beings, our greatness lies not so much in being able to remake the world ... as in being able to remake ourselves."
Mahatma Gandhi

"Just as your car runs more smoothly and requires less energy to go faster and farther when the wheels are in perfect alignment, you perform better when your thoughts, feelings, emotions, goals, and values are in balance."
Brian Tracy

"What you become is more important than what you accomplish."
Anonymous

WHAT ON EARTH HAVE YOU BEEN TOLD?

THIS chapter is a real opportunity to search through those influences from the past and clear out the ones that no longer serve you. What do I mean by this? Well, imagine for moment all the influences that you have ever been exposed to during your life. Imagine all the television, the films, the things people have said, the teachers, the parents, the siblings, the friends, the lovers, the magazines, the books (yes including this one!), everything that has ever passed into your eyes and ears. These influences have created for you a way of seeing the world.

The purpose of this chapter is to realign you with what is really important in your life. You can cut through all the conditioning and reach into your heart to determine what is of value during your lifetime. Then you can use that information to live a wholesome and fulfilling life.

BEING YOURSELF

BEING yourself is the greatest gift you can give to yourself and to others. By doing so, you are suggesting to others that they can do the same. You will not only experience great contentment at finally being your own person, you will also be a guiding light of inspiration to others. You will provide the space in their imagination where they can nurture faith in their own transformation.

We can all grow to our potential. The faith to take bold steps towards that potential can come from many places. Be a source of faith unto yourself while also taking faith from the achievements of others. Then see how a combination of those faiths gives you the courage to step up and become yourself. God is ever patient, demanding nothing. God is pure authenticity:

As God, there is no way you cannot be yourself.

As you learn to *be yourself* you awaken to the fact that you are a celebration of God in form. You will have increased energy, more empowered choice, greater flexibility, better physical health, increased mental speed, and a greater capacity to feel the pleasure as well as the pain of life. Your sensitivity will increase. Your band of experience will widen and expand. Life will be far richer than you have ever known it. Passion for life will erupt from your heart. Your personal choices will ride hand in hand with destiny, manifesting anything you genuinely wish for. Your life will be the life you love. It will be the one you are meant to lead.

CORE VALUES

TO be yourself, you must know your values. Values are amazingly valuable! When you know what your values are, you can do a magical thing: prioritize! Knowing your values means that you spend your life doing things that you really care about, leaving unimportant tasks alone. This is a simple secret to a fulfilling life. It gives you a sense that there is as much time in life as you need, simply because you are using that time to do what is important to you. It is also easy to accept that you cannot do everything at once when you know that you are spending your time doing what really matters to you.

Values that are important to you deserve to be nurtured. But before you can nurture values, you first have to know what they are. They will then come to the forefront of your life. You can only live a life that means something to you when you know what is important to you. I see many people striving to get things that deep down are not very important to them, while they miss out on what it is they truly cherish. This chapter will assist you in avoiding being one of these people, instead becoming someone who transforms their life by knowing their values and acting from that knowledge. You can then live the life that you want, with *your* values at the centre of it. If you do not place your core important values at the centre of your life, then others will put their values there. You will live other peoples' lives until the day you promote your own core values above anyone else's.

Your core values are whatever you need to be yourself, and to become as healthy and powerful as you possibly can. Your core values might include respect, compassion, sharing, trust, communication, honesty, love, passion, challenge, growth, warmth, a beautiful home, good friends or nourishing food. The exercise at the end of this chapter assists you in identifying your core values. Once you have identified them, you can take the exciting step towards honoring them. If you honor your core values and make the choice to allow them more space in your life, then you will find that more and more, your life is *yours*. You will find that it is the life that you love and that you knew you could always lead.

Being in touch with your core values means that you will attract more and more of them into your life. You will naturally choose situations that have more of your core values in them. Likewise, you will avoid situations that are barren of your values. You will be living a life according to what is important to *you*. The alternative is to live your life according to what is important to your society, your parents and your government. Make the switch *now*. Honor those values that are important to you, and sacrifice all those situations that limit those core values.

To get clear about what your core values are, do the exercise below to get clear about this. Then take action to do things according to your core values so that your life is filled with them.

EXERCISE

Write a list of at least twelve things that really matter to you.

Write a list of at least twelve personality aspects of yourself that you rate as essentially important.

Choose your most cherished value from each of the two lists so that you have two values that are massively important to you.

Imagine a future scenario in which these two values are strong and abundant in your life.

Get a feeling in your body about what that will be like. Imagine how you will look, walk, speak and move. Imagine what you can see around you, and what you can hear.

Write a list of ten actions that could lead you to that future. Be specific.

Over the next month, do each of the ten actions. As you do each action, imagine the future scenario you imagined previously and get a sense of that scenario coming closer and closer to you, as if it could happen any minute.

Questions and Answers

Q: I just don't know what is important to me any more. It is all very well talking about core values but how can I know what these are?

A: Look into your heart. What is in your heart is vast. It is the love that you are made of. When you contact that part of you, it becomes clear what is important to you. What you love and what is important to you is exactly the same thing. I once asked people at a seminar to write down a list of things that they loved. When they had finished this, I asked them to write down a list of things that were important to them. They just looked at me blankly. "But they are the same things," they said. Know what you truly love and you will know your core values. Tuning in to your heart's love can be simplified by trial and error. In other words, if you are not sure if you love something in life, try it out. If you enjoy it and it makes you feel like you belong in the world, then you surely do love it. If it makes you feel isolated, disconnected from yourself and miserable, then you don't love it. Don't be afraid to act to find out what you love!

Q: My core values keep changing. For example, twenty years ago I would have said money and sex were my core values. Now I find things like fulfillment and generosity are more important. What is the point of determining my core values if they are going to change over time?

A: What you say is true: core values are subject to change. It is not definite that they will change over time but they may do. The usefulness of knowing your core values is in knowing that becoming clear about their core values than what is important to you right here and now is the essential first step to manifesting it. In other words, until you know what you want you are very unlikely to get it. When you know what you want, however, then you can pull all your resources together to make it happen. I have seen someone with a terminal illness get clear that their number-one priority is getting healthy again. This might sound obvious, but it is often ill people who are most out of touch with their core values. They went on to get better from it. Other remarkable things I have witnessed have been people becoming rich very suddenly or finding a soul mate to settle down with. It is by knowing your core values that you take the first step on the path of attracting it into your life. Then when you have satisfied certain core values, you may experience a change in your value system, thereby sending you off on a new path. We are always in a state of constant change, therefore embracing this state and making the most of it means we can work on what is important to us right here and now.

Personal Story

ONE example of the power of core values to change life can be seen with Carl. He was a middle-aged man with a wiry frame and a wonderful smile. However, he was not feeling great. He complained about not having enough time to do what he really wanted in life, and about always having to work. When I asked him what it is was he really wanted to do in his life, he became confused. "Not working all the time," was as specific as he could be. When we got more specific about this, we found ourselves working with core values. To determine these, I asked him a series of questions: "What do you care about right now?"; "What would you miss most if it was taken away from you?"; "Why are you here? (in my office – this wasn't an existential question!)". This focused him on what was really important in his life. Eventually we had a list of twenty-three things that were important to him. We then went through them and rated them. We found that his health was number one and his family number two, while work ranked eighth, and money only seventeenth. He looked up at me with delight and said, "I realize what I have been doing. I have been working far too much, and what I really want is more time to be fit and healthy, and more time with my wife and kid." He then became very determined to do this. Next time I saw him, he had cut back on overtime at work and was taking the full amount of holidays owed to him to go abroad with his family. He had also joined a gym, started a nutrition program, and put on a healthy amount of weight. He looked much fresher and happier, still with that inimitable smile. While he unconsciously knew what his values were, he did not have the consciousness to do anything about them, until we got down to the basics: what was important to him!

6

KNOW YOUR BOUNDARIES

"We must learn our limits. We are all something, but none of us are everything."
Blaise Pascal

"To trust yourself to test your limits. That is the courage to succeed."
Bernard Edmonds

"Never give up your right to be wrong, because then you will lose the ability to learn new things and to move forward with your life."
Dr. David M. Burns

"The only limit to our realization of tomorrow will be our doubts of today."
Franklin D. Roosevelt

Feeling The Edges

EVERYONE has limits. The ability to be free is to know and respect these limits. While this may sound like a contradiction, think of it this way: if you have only a limited number of things you can do, then you are free to choose what, how and when you do those things. Take the example of a career: you might have four or five careers that really excite you. This makes it easier to make a dedicated choice to pursue one of them. Imagine if you had a million options. Where would you start?

Getting specific about your vocation is just one way of experiencing the usefulness of knowing your boundaries. Another way is to be aware of the limits of your body. So many people in these times are using their bodies in a way that does not suit them. Mobile phones, damaged fats in food, long periods of sitting, driving instead of walking: all these things have contributed to a society that has become disconnected from their body (see the chapter entitled "Empower Your Body" for more details on how to become reconnected). There is basically a lack of respect for the limits of the body.

Like all forms, the body is limited. Obviously, you know that you cannot jump unaided into the air to a height of 50 meters, but physical limits are much more subtle than that, for example the point at which a body is in need of water. Being aware of such physical limits is a route to lasting health.

When you know the way the world works and understand that all form is limited by its very nature, then you can use those forms in a way that makes them very useful. For example, the mind has limitations – it cannot easily understand the usual paradoxes of life that are commonly experienced, such as how you can be happy and sad at the same time. It cannot fully understand why you love someone or something. Nor can it be relied upon to give you accurate data one hundred percent of the time, especially when trying to remember the contents of a conversation from two months ago. When you know what the mind can do and cannot do, then you can use it much more wisely. It becomes an aid and assistant to carrying out the actions of your heart's path. It can plan, imagine, and calculate on your heart's behalf to get results that are meaningful and fulfilling.

When you get specific like this about something very important, like the function of your own mind, you start to determine what something is capable of and then how to use it. Where there is a true respect for boundary and ability, the maximum performance can be obtained from it. For example, an international athlete I coached told me that she was not winning races because of her mental attitude. Now, the term "mental attitude" is very vague. In fact it means different things to different people. But when we got down to specifics, it turned out she was saying to herself inside her head that she was not able to beat her competitors. Now, that is something tangible. I could more easily relate to what she meant as soon as she was specific. Furthermore, because she got specific, we could do something about it. We could not do anything about "mental attitude" but we could do something about the way she talked to herself in her head. So we changed the way she talked in her head during race meetings and she started winning races.

Trust is Easy When You Have Solid Boundaries

NOT only does our mental attitude improve when we know our boundaries, but so does our relationships with other people. Relationships need trust and security in them if they are to be sustainable. Trust and security can only be built when both parties in a relationship are aware of where their boundaries lie.

Boundaries in this sense mean the psychological limitations of an individual's personality. Boundaries literally contain us as people. They may change and shift, but wherever they are they define our personality. They mark the outer edges of our personality, much like the skin marks the outer edges of our body. Imagine what life would be like if we were not aware of the outer edges of our body. We would constantly collide with things around us. We would bump into other people. We wouldn't be able to execute tasks effectively. In short, we would be in conflict with our environment, with others around us, and ultimately with ourselves.

Yet it is exactly the same with psychological boundaries. If we are not aware where they lie, then that lack of awareness would create conflict in our lives. We would be bumping into things and other people, not physically but emotionally and psychologically.

We only have a strong sense of personal security when we know where our boundaries lie. One of the greatest sources of insecurity is not being sure where our psychological perimeters are. Where does your personality end and the rest of the world begin? The answer to this is essential if you are to live in a relationship with another without getting sucked into *becoming them* or living in *conflict with them*. When this happens, relationships become a struggle to get *away* from the other to achieve the missing independence. This is often mixed with a strong pull *towards* the other in the hope that psychological boundaries can be reclaimed by being with the other. So begins the push-pull struggle that ultimately detracts from the sustainability of relationships.

You must be self-contained in order to effectively share your life with another. And how can you share yourself with another if you do not know what "yourself" is? A strong sense of boundaries is essential to letting people come in to share your personal space. It is only when you have boundaries that you can choose to let them down and invite another to come within them. Without boundaries, you cannot choose who comes into your space and when they come into it. You do not have the power of control over who you share your personal space with. This means that you will feel over-vulnerable and the experience of sharing your life with another will often feel like being invaded. You will constantly defend yourself from such an "invasion" by pushing people away. This pushing away is an attempt to make boundaries when it is too late to do so as someone has already come into yourpersonal space.

The following exercise focuses you on how to be clear about your boundaries and how to protect yourself from unwanted influences in your life, thereby allowing you to be more open to those influences you do want. Take a few moments to try the following:

EXERCISE

Write a list of all the things in your life that you are no longer willing to tolerate. Include all those things that you have quietly allowed to happen in your life that you really are not comfortable with.

Take the first thing on the list, close your eyes, and visualize it as an object separate from you. For example, if you are no longer willing to tolerate betrayal from friends, then you could visualize a person to represent a friend betraying you.

Next, visualize yourself drawing a colored line between you and that object. This symbolizes your boundary.

Next, imagine that the object is trying to get closer to you by getting past the line you imagined.

Become aware of what you need to do to make sure that the object goes back and stays out of your space. Be aware of any emotions or actions that assist with this.

Finally, imagine what this means in the real world – how can you make new actions that will help you to protect your boundaries? What will you have to say or do to make it clear to others where your limits lie? When will you do this?

Do these steps for each item on your list, until you have an arsenal of new behaviors and strategies for keeping undesirable influences out of your personal space.

Questions and Answers

Q: All my life, I feel as if I haven't spoken out when things have been uncomfortable. I just kept quiet and hoped things would go away. I feel terrified at the prospect of getting angry with someone, so I never do. I often leave situations feeling unfairly treated. How can I change these habits after such a long time of pleasing other people?

A: It is essential for you to connect anger to communication. Anger is a very real and beautiful emotion. It serves to protect your boundaries from negative influences that may cause damage to your mind, body or other emotions. Anger is like the big brother that comes to look after you when you have been unfairly treated. The challenge with anger is to express it in the moment that you feel it. When you learn to do this, scary as it may be at first, you will break the habit of a lifetime. When anger is expressed in the moment it is felt, it can come out in ways that are non-violent. In other words, you get to make clear your boundaries without suppressing anger. Suppressed anger can be very dangerous. Most of us have encountered a person who seems massively irritated by something that is essentially trivial. This kind of behavior is a sign of suppressed anger bubbling to the surface. Ironically, expressing anger directly and without malice is a path to intimacy. It is only when we are clear about our boundaries that others know how to respect them. Where boundaries are not clearly defined, distance grows between people. You have to be clear about your boundaries to others so that they can show you respect. This is a way of showing love, and therefore will bring you closer together. The fear of doing this may be very strong and very real but it does not have to stop you doing it. You have the ultimate choice.

Q: I find that other people define my boundaries for me most of the time. It really annoys me. I try to make my boundaries clear but then I feel guilty as if it is not fair to be asking for what I want. So then I stop myself and step back into line. This means that what I do with my life is controlled by those around me, and not by me. My work and my family seem like a trap, and I wish they weren't. How can I reconcile this?

A: What you are describing is the way that most of the world lives right now. This is why there is so much disillusionment with working life and why marriages and family values break up so often. It is very empowering that you are aware that it doesn't have to be this way. When we live according to someone else's plan, we live a life that is half-dead. Your destiny is hidden in your heart. It is in the heart that you will find your true path on the planet. When you deeply love your life, you will find yourself inside your destiny. This may correlate to someone else's idea of your life purpose or it may not. Either way, if you stay true to your own destiny, you will live a fulfilling life in which the love that resides within you is witnessed as being all around you on the outside of your life – in your work, in your family, in your relationships, in the trees, in the sky, in the cars, in the way someone smiles at you – then life cannot seem like a trap. Then life becomes a celebration. Life is an amazing opportunity to appreciate the immense beauty and wonder of the universe. To get out of feeling trapped in your life, it may be helpful to appreciate what makes you what you are (see the Exercise in the earlier chapter entitled Experience Uniqueness). Then you may be clear that no one on planet Earth is made the same way you are. Therefore, the way that you do things is going to be different to the way others do them. With this as your starting point, you can see that what you do in life is really down to your choice, and yours alone. Others may have an investment in you being a certain way because they are getting something from you, e.g. your husband and children may want you to remain the way you are because then they can mould you to do what they want. The same may be true at work. Your boss and work colleagues will have a vested interested in you remaining the same. However, it is crucial for your own self-respect to honor your boundaries, even when this means you upset the status quo. Remember this: the happiest, most successful people in the world respect their boundaries. They get to live life the way they want, and this means they have greater energy to succeed in whatever area of life they choose. So, take a leap of faith and tell people what you want to do and why. Then DO IT. Let others deal with their own emotional responses. Of course, you can still be there for your family and workplace, but in a new way: liberated, more energized and ultimately more effective. Ultimately you will be happier when you look after yourself while making it clear to others what you need in order to do that.

Personal Story

ROWAN is a tall, smartly dressed man who owns his own home, and works as a private chef. He has spent his life looking after his wife and family, and working long hours in a very demanding job. All in the same year, his wife announced that she wanted a divorce, and his doctor told him he had prostrate cancer. He was forced to re-evaluate his entire life. When he came to me he was very confused and didn't know what to do. While we worked on many areas, the greatest reassessment of his life was in defining his boundaries. Since he was not reading his body's signals very well, he was overworking and causing himself unnecessary stress. This was all in an attempt, we discovered, to elicit love from his family for the things he did, rather than by who he was. As this is a very common malaise for men to find themselves with, we worked to unravel his habit of doing what he believed others wanted him to. We went back to basics, and got him in touch with his body to find out what was needed there. The signals were clear – heal the cancer and relax more often. Then we worked on the boundaries of his working life. He said that he had worked so hard so that his family would love him. During our coaching relationship, he discovered that his son and daughter did actually love him for who he was. He was then able to honor a boundary in his life that he was never able to in the past: to work in way that did not cause undue stress to the body. He took a strong stance and decided to ease off on the work, even considering leaving his job altogether. Then we moved on to boundaries in his life like his lifestyle. He said that he needed more social contact outside of his family but had never made this clear, so had tried artificially to fit into the family boundaries instead of honoring his own.

    He set about creating new boundaries for himself so that he could socialize more often. This included joining local clubs, meeting friends, and letting his family do their own housework. With all this change in circumstance, Rowan was able to reconfigure his life to better the reflect the true desires of his heart, rather than fitting in to what he perceived his family would want him to do. His family have all been very supportive in these changes, even his wife. Although she still wants a divorce, she too is happy that at last he is defining his own limits. By doing so, he is better able to live the life he really wants and get his physical health back on an even keel.

7

KNOW YOUR FEARS

"Do the thing you fear to do and keep on doing it ... that is the quickest and surest way ever yet discovered to conquer fear."
Dale Carnegie

"Love is what we were born with. Fear is what we learn. The spiritual journey is the unlearning of fear and the acceptance of love back into our hearts."
Marianne Williamson

"Fear leads to anger. Anger leads to hate. Hate leads to the Dark Side."
Yoda

"Courage is knowing what to fear."
Plato

What Has Fear Become?

FEAR is a very useful emotion: it keeps us alive. None of us would be alive today without the emotion of fear. Imagine if you walked close to a cliff edge or a busy road without the emotion of fear to keep you alert and concerned. You would not last long. But why, if fear is useful, has it become such an obstacle to people living the life they really want? The answer is simple: fear has been given the power to determine actions even when it is a very slight fear.

Fear can only override your actions and prevent you from doing something if it is very strong basic survival fear, such as the kind mentioned previously that you may feel by a cliff or a road. This kind of fear has an ability to override our actions and pull us back from the cliff or road. However, other fears do not carry such a strong survival message. Some fears are not threatening to our life: the fear of getting a new job, the fear of moving house, the fear of leaving a relationship, the fear of being in a relationship, the fear of being angry with someone, the fear of calling someone who you don't like, the fear of being who you really want to be. These are not basic survival issues. Rather they are choices that you can make without threatening the survival of the physical body. And yet, these fears can stop you doing the things you want to do in life. However, the good news is:

Those fears can only stop you doing what you want when you allow them as much power over your actions as the fear of death.

Sounds irrational, doesn't it? That you might stop yourself getting a new job in case you die, or you might stop yourself being in a relationship because it might leave you dead? And yet this is what is preventing millions of people around the world from living life to their fullest potential. In this chapter, we will explore the different kinds of fear, what to do when you feel fear, and a few little-known secrets as to how to reduce your fear levels so that life is made easier.

Fearing Change

IT is an amazing thing that you can become fearful of something that is actually beneficial to you. When something new is about to happen, fear can often rear its head. Although it is misplaced, it seems very real. But the question is, what is this fear trying to tell you? Is it telling you to pay closer attention to what you are about to do or is it warning you that you will damage yourself by doing this action?

Fears of progressing in life are nearly always there simply to get you to pay more attention to what you are doing. In other words, you get fearful as a way of making yourself focus on the task at hand. That is why this mild kind of fear is very common when important things are being undertaken. The fear was never meant to breed distrust or prevent you from achieving your goals. It is just a friendly reminder that change is happening and to be alert to any potential dangers.

Given the choice, everyone I know would choose a more enjoyable and more empowered life. However, it is fear that so often stops those people from actually living in this way. Fear can prevent positive things happening to you. Have you ever wanted to do something you knew would help you grow and prosper but were too fearful to do it? When this happens, it is useful to be conscious that the fear is *misplaced*. To move through the fear, you must see the fear for what it is, and then take the first step in the direction you wish to go. This first step is usually the most challenging. With that taken, the others follow more easily. If you are sure that the direction you are taking is a positive and beneficial one for you, then you can use the techniques described in this chapter to find a resourceful courage within you to take the first step.

The four main fears that prevent the manifestation of a successful and passionate life are the fear of success, the fear of failure, the fear of rejection and the fear of abandonment.

A. *Fear of success*

The fear of success has its roots in two other fears: the fear of responsibility and the fear of connectivity. If you are successful, you will be in demand from others. If you do not have the responsibility to look after your own needs, then looking after the needs of others can seem very scary. Also, with success comes the opportunity for a deeper connection with other people. Because success carries with it the flame of achievement, people feel better about themselves when they are successful. Feeling good about yourself makes both business and personal relationships easier. You do not have to hide yourself in shame, and can express yourself fully no matter who you are with.

Because people are attracted to others that are successful, you will need to be ready to stretch your ability to be responsible and to be connected to others. To overcome any fear of becoming successful, you must first grow in your capacity for responsibility and connectivity. You must take the stance that says "I am responsible for my life and I welcome connections with other people into it". Only then can success seem like an attractive, non-threatening option.

Deep down we all want to succeed in our work. We may want to achieve something particular (like selling a painting or doing a course), or we may want to achieve something long term (like being a good parent or earning massive financial wealth). Success is so much easier if we are ready for it. If not, then even if it happens we may find ourselves so afraid that we do not enjoy it and it complicates our life.

Overcoming the fear of success is perhaps the single most important hurdle for you to jump on your way to a successful life. This may take perseverance, which means you don't give up the first, second, or third time your life path doesn't feel good or rewarding to you. You persevere until it does.

My definition of courage is "letting your heart direct your actions". Moving with courage will naturally unblock any fear-based obstructions to your success. If you want success then do not be deterred by a little fear. Remember, fear is a warning sign and is an ally. It is just that sometimes it shows up in inappropriate places.

B. *Fear of failure*

Fear of failing is given to us by the schooling system and in many cases by parents. Children are continually punished for failing and valued for their successes. They therefore link success with love and link failure with lack of love. The child's ability to fail then becomes reduced. This means that it is difficult to achieve the results that are desired. This is because:

Success depends on the ability to fail.

Successful people fail a lot. They know how to fail, and are not afraid to do it. If you try something once and it fails so you decide you will never do it again, then you have ensured you will never succeed at it.

Failure is a learning mechanism that it is essential to success. If you attempt to satisfy a desire, then it is natural that sometimes you will fail. This is not a problem until it is judged as being wrong. Failing is not wrong, unless you are perfect. The problem with perfect people is that they never fail.

Perfectionism is simply a yearning for everything to be so completely under control that mistakes are never made and failure never results. Perfectionism may seem attractive on the surface. However in my seminars I occasionally ask the question, "If you could have everything go perfectly for you all the time would you?" Most people say, "Of course," or "You bet!" Then I ask people to think about what it would really be like. A lot of people guess it would be intensely enjoyable for a few weeks or even a few months. However, when people really consider it, they usually see that perfection would be a nightmare. If everything were perfect, then you would no longer know the difference between failure and success. Life would become a bland sequence of repetitive happenings. Success is only sweet because of failures.

When you experience failure, you get to learn what success is. The greatest talent in building a successful life is to persevere during failure. Later in the book we will look at designing the goals for your life that will guide you to where you want to be. We shall also see that those who have successful lives do so by establishing their life goals and persevering in the accomplishment of them.

Do not limit your life goals according to fear of failure. If you accept your failures and learn from them, then you will always succeed. To overcome fear of failure, imagine something that you would really love to do but find a little frightening to do. To begin with, choose something you are mildly scared of. Then, just do it. While you are doing it, watch what happens to the fear. Do you feel it any more? How do you feel having stepped through the fear and accomplished something you love? Once a small step has been taken, try something that is more scary for you. Then progress to that major step that you have wanted to make for many years but have been too afraid to take. If you take that step, you may accomplish the success of doing something that your heart loves.

C. Fear of rejection

Whenever you do something you really believe in, you run the risk of it being rejected by others. Will what you do be accepted and appreciated? Or will it be rejected and sneered at? It is totally unknown whether this will happen until you take the step to actually do it. The fear of rejection can paralyze a person to the point where they never take that first step towards doing something that their heart loves. Just as success needs failure as a counterbalance, so acceptance needs rejection.

Get one thing clear before embarking upon your life of heartfelt courage: what you do will occasionally be rejected. No one ever formed a successful life without taking some knocks. The main difference between those who achieve successful lives and those who do not is the level of perseverance. If we are told by one person that what we do is not wanted, do we quit or continue? This is the crossroads where you can take the road to success through perseverance or take the road to self-limitation by quitting.

You need to fortify your convictions to achieve success. This includes understanding this:

A rejection of what you do is not a rejection of *who you are*.

Imagine that what you do is a musical note and what you are is a musician. Your musical note is one among many in the music. Now imagine that your note is superfluous to requirements. Imagine that while it may fit in another tune, it does not fit in this one. It is therefore rejected *because it is not appropriate*. This is no reflection on the quality of the note; rather it is a sign that circumstances are not right for the note's acceptance. Furthermore, the rejection of the note is no reflection on the quality of you as a musician. It is the note that is being rejected, *not* the creator of the note.

If you are objective about what you do in life, you will see that you and your creations are separate entities. This objectivity gives you the confidence to strike out and follow the life you wish without fearing the rejection of your self. Most successful people see rejection as circumstantial rather than as a reflection on their own worth.

Self-worth is the key to overcoming the fear of rejection. When you value yourself, you may feel disappointed if you are rejected but you'll retain awareness that it is to do with circumstances and not with the value of your contribution. It is this feeling of self-worth which gives you the confidence to follow your heart without the fear of rejection paralyzing you. The next exercise is designed to remind you of your self-worth.

EXERCISE

Sit with closed eyes and reflect upon your life. Try to remember all the events within it that made you feel good about your self, worthy about yourself, or valued by others.

Next, write them down in a list.

Now, look through the list and tick any of them that

are especially strong or striking in terms of their ability to inspire confidence.

Answer these questions for each item that you ticked:
1. What was it that made me feel good about myself?
2. Do I want to repeat these circumstances again and again?

Find the items that you answered "yes" to for Question 2. Write a list of actions you can take that will create these kind of circumstances in your life. Give each action a date by which it will be completed.

Do those actions by the dates you chose.

D. Fear of Abandonment

The fear of abandonment is rooted deeply in your survival mechanisms. As a baby, your fear of abandonment kept you alive. You cried out if this fear got too strong, thereby letting your mother know that attention was needed. The fear is that, "if mother goes, I will die", which for a baby may be true. For all the baby knows, it would die if its mother left. The baby learns to use the fear of abandonment to prevent abandonment from happening and therefore to protect themselves from death. We must fear abandonment to survive as babies. This is a primal mechanism, rooted in the very depths of survival.

What happens as you grow up is that you no longer require fear of abandonment as a survival mechanism. As you develop the ability to take care of your own needs, you learn to trust that your needs will be taken care of. If this growth was interrupted, then as an adult you will continue to use fear of abandonment as a survival mechanism. This produces a block to the development of a living a truly inspiring life. If your actions are controlled by a fear of abandonment then you will be deprived of the physical, mental, and emotional energy necessary to create a successful life.

To overcome fear of abandonment, you must nurture practice meeting your own needs, thereby building the trust that they will be met in the future. To help develop your ability to meet your own needs, do the following exercise:

EXERCISE

Write a two-column list. In the first column, write down any needs that you feel are not being met at present. In the second column, write down any needs that you currently feel you are meeting well.

Read through the needs that you are currently meeting well and in each case write down how you are accomplishing this.

Next, read through the needs you feel are not being met at present. For each unmet need, devise an action that will take you closer to meeting it. Again, give each action a date by which you will do it.

Finally (as always) take the action!

Only by being active and courageous will fear diminish enough for you to pursue the life goals you wish for and deserve. To nurture trust that your needs will be taken care of, you can keep a check on day-to-day events where it appears "luck" has manifested. Luck is the harmonization of your needs and wants with events around you. It is also something that can be created by you when you develop the maturity and ability to take care of your own needs and wants.

When you meet your needs like this it can bring home the fact that *all is at hand.* Everything is taken care of *for* you in the vastness of God's destiny, and everything is taken care of *by* you in your detailed individual life choices.

WHAT IS FEAR ANYWAY?

To feel an emotion we must feel it in the body.
This means that every emotion we have manifests as an internal sensation in the body. Often this feeling is located in a certain area. When you feel fear, if you pay close attention to your body, you will find that the sensation of fear is located in one or more areas of your body. Often people will report to me that they feel fear in the abdomen or in the head, or in the neck. Sometimes people feel fear in more than one place. Occasionally people will feel fear all over their body. The other thing to note about emotions is:
If you can feel an emotion, it must be moving in your body.
So to feel fear in the body, not only must you have a location but you must also have a movement to that emotion. For example it may be a contraction, a spinning sensation, or a lurching sensation. Perhaps it has a temperature, for example warm, cool, hot, or cold.

When they know these things, most people can identify the location and movement of fear in their body. They can describe to me where they are feeling fear and what that fear moves like in their body. There are literally as many ways that an emotion can move in the body as there are ways that things can move outside of the body. I have had reports of emotions moving like sparkling light on the sea, like a pendulum, and like a clenched fist.

When you know where your fear is in your body and how it moves, you are already at an advantage. You are *in touch* with your fear. This means you are empowered by the knowledge of what it is. For example, knowing that your fear is a contraction around the abdomen allows you to change that feeling by relaxing your abdomen. When you know your fear, it releases its vice-like grip over your actions. You become free to do what you love without having to stop yourself because of an unknown entity called "fear".

I would like to share with you a secret that sounds so obvious yet when you use it, the results are amazing:

A very slight lack of air, water or nutrients in your body can cause fear.

If the body has even a tiny lack of what it needs, then it will go into a state of biological shock. This can be caused by a small lack of: deeply breathed clean air, regular intake of pure water, or water-rich whole foods. To survive, the body produces fear in an attempt to motivate action. What often happens is that the body is ignored, and the fear of survival is translated to a person's daily life. Their work, finances or relationships can all be affected.

The body needs you to listen to it. If you do not listen, then the body does not get what it needs. Fear becomes more and more likely, as the emotional response to that neglect. Listen to your body and give it what it needs. Breathe clean air deeply, drink 2–4 liters of water a day and ensure you have a good intake of green foods, vitamins and minerals. Then your body will trust you. When your body trusts you it will produce internal sensations that then create emotions of trust, happiness and goodwill.

EXERCISE

Think of a time when you really wanted to do something but stopped yourself because you were fearful. It could be anything, for example, asking someone on a date, applying for a new job, or talking to someone in authority.

Close your eyes and imagine yourself to be back there. See what you could see then, hear what you could hear then, and feel what it felt like back then.

Get a sense of any feelings of fear. Ask yourself these two questions:
1. Where is the feeling of fear located in my body?
2. How does the feeling of fear move in my body?

Next, choose a time in your life when you were afraid to do something but you did it anyway. Think hard until you remember a time.

Now close your eyes again and imagine yourself at that time. Get a sense of what it looked like, what is sounded like, and what it felt like back then. Get a clear sense of what it was like at that time.

Get a sense of any feelings you had at that time. What feelings were they? Where were they located? How did they move?

Close your eyes again, and remember again the time when you were too scared to do what you wanted to do.

This time, however, I would like you to try this: slowly change the movement of the fear to the movement you felt when you did something you were scared of. So if the movement of fear was a contraction inwards, and the movement of accomplishing something is an expansion outwards, then change the movement from a contraction to an expansion. You may be surprised how easy it is to do this.

Next, change the location too. So if the fear was in the abdomen, and the feeling of doing something that you were scared of is in the chest area then move the feeling up to the chest.

You should be left over with the feeling of doing something you are scared of, but still have the sight and/or sounds of the time you could not do anything.

Notice how differently you feel about that situation now. Imagine yourself doing what you were scared of, now that you have the feeling that you can.

QUESTIONS AND ANSWERS

Q: I am very scared of public speaking. Whenever I talk in groups of people my hands get sweaty and my heart misses beats. I get so worried, I can't think straight. I often stutter or my words come out wrong. Why does this happen? What can I do to change this?

A: Fear like this is associative. This means that you get scared because of a previous time in your life. Some time in the past you got scared while public speaking. Now, every time you try to speak publicly, you feel scared. It is likely that at some time you were forced to stand up and speak in front of others when you were feeling uncomfortable. This then set up a pattern so you will feel this way every time you speak publicly. Difficulty with things like speaking, and writing are usually rooted in a school system that does not respect or understand the emotions of children. But the good news is you that your future does not equal your past! You can change this response. After all, the response is *involuntary*. You do not get on to stage thinking, "Come on, now is the time to get scared." It just happens automatically – an unconscious behavior pattern. By remembering a time that you were very confident doing something, you can learn how you felt that time. You can then teach your unconscious how to adopt this new way of feeling when you next speak in front of others. Use the exercise in this chapter to install this new way of behaving into your unconscious.

Q: Whenever I see a woman I am attracted to, I become very worried. I start thinking that she will not like me, and say to myself that she will not be interested in me. This makes me scared to talk to her, let alone ask her on date. What can I do?

A: There is an amazing thing that when you learn, it can change your whole perspective of how much power you really have: **You create the fear that you feel.**

This means that fear is not something that is created outside of you but is engineered within you and it is engineered in the body. How you make fear will vary on the circumstance, but from what you have said it is clear that you have a number of steps to your behavior. First you see a woman, then you talk to yourself in way that creates a feeling of fear in the body. You can do this easily. Think of it this way: if you wanted to create a feeling of fear for yourself, you could simply look at a car driving along a road, then say to yourself that a person in this car is going try to kill you. If you did this convincingly, you would produce a feeling of fear in the body. In other words, you would scare yourself. This is exactly what you are doing with these women! You are seeing something then saying to yourself that they will not like you, then feeling fear. If you didn't say these things to yourself, you would not feel the fear. Luckily, you can change the content your thinking. For example, you could replace the thought "they will not be interested in me." with the song 'Happy Birthday' or a recap of today's weather. Alternatively, you could change the location and movement of the feeling that is produced by using the previous exercise.

Personal Story

JAMES was a tanned, well-traveled man in his fifties. He came to me because he said he was unable to dance and that it was a source of great discomfort and annoyance to him. He asked me to do something that would enable him to dance once more. It was obvious his body was capable of it since he was not restricted in movement, so I enquired as to the last time he danced. He said it was when he was eleven at a school disco. Everyone was doing "the twist", a popular dance of that era. Surprisingly, his teacher stopped the music and made James do the twist in front of the entire school. She then told him he was hopeless and not dancing properly. One can only imagine at the immense amount of shame and embarrassment bestowed upon James in that moment. He never danced again. He said that he always felt terrible whenever the opportunity to dance presented itself, and he would always make excuses as to why he wasn't dancing. Obviously, this was not helping his relationships with the ladies. When I took James back to that memory, he could vividly see the school disco. In his mind, he could hear the music and his teacher talking to him. He could also feel a feeling of trauma in his body. When I asked him to identify that feeling, he said it was the fear and shame of being shown up in front of the whole school. I asked where in his body it was and how it moved. He said it was in his stomach and chest and moved in a clockwise circle. I asked him if he could slow down the circling motion and he said he could. We got him to slow it down to a stop, and then moved on to a confident memory. He remembered a time he was scared of something but did it anyway. He remembered a time when he went sailing and got swept offshore. He kept telling himself that he had to get back to the shore no matter what. He told himself that he couldn't let the fear stop him. I got him to remember how that felt and he described it as a rising sensation coming from his chest through his head, then upwards and outwards through the top of his head. Then, I got him to go back to the school disco memory. He closed his eyes and imagined himself back there. He stopped the spinning circle, then made it go upwards out of his head. Then we got him to make sure it started at his chest and was not in his stomach anymore. When he had done all this, he found that he was feeling the courageous attitude he had when sailing and could now feel that way while remembering the school disco incident. After that, James was able to dance publicly. After a gap of over forty years, he was at last able to so something that he was once too afraid to contemplate. By using the principle that people make their own emotions out of the experiences around them, he was able to transfer a positive experience into a different area of his life.

PART 3

EMPOWER YOURSELF

Part 3 is a journey into empowerment. In the next three chapters, you will learn what your mind, body and emotions are made up of, how to care for them so that they stay healthy, and what to do when things go wrong. When you empower these three 'vehicles' then you will have greater energy to devote to improving your life.

8

EMPOWER YOUR MIND

"Most people are about as happy as they make up their minds to be."
Abraham Lincoln

"Don't limit yourself. Many people limit themselves to what they think they can do. You can go as far as you mind lets you. What you believe, you can achieve."
Mary Kay Ash

"Real difficulties can be overcome; it is only the imaginary ones that are unconquerable."
Theodore N. Vail

"Anybody can do anything that he imagines."
Henry Ford

The Structure of the Mind

PEOPLE usually think in pictures or in sound. This means that they will get a thought that is either a mental picture or an inner sound. For example, if you think of visiting a friend, you may visualize their face or you may say to yourself "I'd like to visit Bob soon." The former is a picture, the latter is a sound. Sometimes, people think in both pictures and sound, for example imagining a car journey by remembering the inside of the car *and* the sound of the engine.

When you know the way that you think, you have more control over your thoughts. If you are to truly empower the mind, you need to know what thoughts are made up of.

We all have ten senses. You are familiar with the first five as these are our outer senses that we use to gauge the world around us. They are sight, hearing, touch, taste and smell. The second five, however, are often left out of traditional teaching. These senses are the internal versions of the five senses: our inner sight, inner hearing, inner touch, inner taste, and inner smell. You know when a sense is inner or outer because the outer senses all rely on a material object being present to stimulate them, whereas an inner sense can be stimulated without the specific outer object being present. An example of outer sight is seeing your house when you come home. An example of inner sight is remembering the house you lived in as a child. In the first example, you have to be present at your house for the experience, whereas in the second example you can be anywhere. Seeing your childhood home is an internal visualization. This is the way many think.

I regularly ask people during my coaching sessions, "How do you think that?" Often the response is "I don't know." Sometimes I ask them a different way like, "How do you know you had that thought?" People generally take thought for granted and see no reason why they should find out how they are thinking a certain way. Traditionally therapies have concentrated on *why* a certain thought is being formed. My system, *Enhance*™, looks at *how* a thought is made.

Rooting Out Incongruent Thought

EVERYONE has had times in their life when they have been told they cannot do something. Some people may have been shown this in no uncertain terms. The fact is that as children we are vulnerable to learning the thought patterns that others use to judge us. We adopt the very thoughts that others project onto us. A mother might yell at you, "You are no good for anything!" and if your emotional charge is high enough, you will unconsciously adopt that way of talking to yourself in the future. Similarly if you were told, "You can accomplish anything you want," then you will unconsciously adopt that thought pattern.

The thoughts that disturb a person are always the same: they are the ones that are incongruent with their true nature. They are simply not in keeping the flow of God as it moves through their heart. This means that *who* a person really is and *what* a person loves to do are not reflected in their thought patterns. For example, a person may want to feel loved and comfortable, yet their thoughts tell them that they can never achieve this. This is incongruent. Obviously, if thoughts are congruent with what you love they will not disturb you. I congratulate you if all your thoughts are like this. If they are not, or some are not, then this chapter can show you how to transform that state without lengthy exercises, therapy or learning. If you think, "Sounds too good to be true!" then ask yourself how you created that thought. Did you say it in your mind, or did you make a picture? Can you make a picture or say something in your mind that tells you, "I can gain more and more control over my mind?"

Transforming Thought

ONCE you have identified exactly how you make a thought then you can begin to deconstruct it and replace it with another kind of thinking. This then becomes remembered by the body by repeatedly acting on the new way of thinking.

To begin replacing a certain kind of thinking with another, imagine a thought that you regularly have and that you wish you could change. Notice whether the thought is made by picturing something or hearing something inside you. When you know what it is made of, notice the distinct characteristics of the picture or the sound. For example, the picture might be especially light, colorful, drab, fast-moving, or still. You might see yourself in the picture or it might be seen as if through your eyes. With sound, notice whose voice is talking. Is it yours or someone else's? Notice whether it is soft or harsh, loud or quiet, continuous or interrupted. Once you have identified the specific characteristics of the thought, you know what it is made of in great detail.

Now, you can transform it. But what do you want to transform it to? You do not want to make it worse, that is for sure! Also, you probably do not want to adopt an unreal positive thought that has nothing to do with your life. What is most inspiring, and luckily for you also the easiest to implement, is to take a thought pattern from an area of your life that is empowering and uplifting and use that as the replacement. To do this, simply remember a time when you were thinking the way you want to think.

At a one of my seminars we had a woman who thought she couldn't be loved by her partner. She also told me that she knew her partner did love her. I asked her to think of a time when she felt loved. At first she claimed she had never had that thought, but with more questioning we discovered that she felt very loved by her cat. So we used the thoughts she had about her cat.

So, remember a time that you did think the way you wanted. Once you have that, do the same thing as before: close your eyes, and remember thinking that way in great detail, noticing the different characteristics of the thought.

You should end up with two thoughts: the old one that you want to change, and the new one that you want to change to. Then all that you need to do is to change the old one to the new one. This is how to do it: close your eyes, and remember the old thought. If it is a picture and the new thought is too, then change the characteristics of the old one to the characteristics of the new one. For example, if the woman's picture of her cat was bright and the one of her partner was dark, she would make the one of her partner bright too. What this does is tell the unconscious that you are adopting a new way of thinking. Doing this process without distractions is important. The more you focus on doing this without interruption and in a very relaxing place, the better the results will be.

If you had a sound for the old thought and a sound for the new one, then change the old thought with the new characteristics. So if your old thought was your dad's voice and your new one is your own voice, say the same thing but in your voice. If the old one is a sound and the new one a picture then turn down the volume of the sound to zero and fade up the picture.

It is easy to do this. If you doubt that it is, imagine the front door of your house. Now imagine it is painted an entirely different color, red for instance. You have just changed a thought. Now try it with sound. Close your eyes and imagine your mother's voice in your head. Now imagine her voice being very high pitched as if she has breathed from a helium balloon. Again, you have changed a characteristic of a thought without changing the content of it. You see how easy it is to think of the door while changing the color of it. It is exactly the same process with the old and new thoughts. Simply take the old thought and change the characteristics of it with the new one.

CHANGE THE THOUGHT, CHANGE THE FEELING

IN my experience, when someone wants to change a thought it is because of the feeling the thought creates in them. Therefore, you will know whether your change of thinking has been successful by the results you get in your body. You will remember from the previous chapter that all emotion gets felt in the body. So the body is the touchstone of success in the above technique. If you have generated new feelings like empowerment, love and joy then you have succeeded. Listen to the body and you will find out. The exercise is listed again in brief below. Learning and use it to gain essential mastery over the mind, so that it become a true ally. Try the exercise first with something of low emotional consequence (like thoughts of despair at cleaning your house). Then build up until you can change the thought patterns that disturb you the most. That way, you will learn the method before entering it to the full power of it.

Exercise

Choose a thought pattern that you want to transform.

Close your eyes and remember thinking that way. Is it a picture? If so, is it bright or dark? Colorful or dull? Moving or still? Can you see yourself in the picture or are you seeing it through your eyes? Is it a sound? If it is a voice, is it your voice or someone else's? Is it soft or harsh? Quiet or loud? Continuous or interrupted?

Choose a new empowering thought pattern that you want to put in its place.

Ask yourself the same questions about this new thought.

Finally, change the characteristics of the old thought with the characteristics of your new thought.

Questions and Answers

Q: Whenever I try to remember thinking a certain way, I draw a blank so I cannot do what you asking. How can I jog my memory?
A: Remembering how the actual thought form is created is the best way of accomplishing this technique but it is not the only way. You

can also just think of the time and place where you know you were thinking in that way. Close your eyes and simply see what saw then, hear what you heard then, and feel what you felt then. Now you have a picture and/or sound to work with. Do the same for the new empowering thought. Remember the time and place it happened and concentrate on the scene around you rather than the actual thought form itself. Now you can use the characteristics from these scenes rather from the thoughts within the scenes.

Q: I am having trouble making the changes. I see characteristics from one of the memories and try to apply to it to the other but can't get it to stick. It always seems to change back again afterwards. In day-to-day life, the effect of this is that I get a change in my thinking for a day or two then the old pattern comes back. How do I get it to stay?

A: This is a great question. How do we make changes stick? Firstly, check that you are being specific enough with the characteristics. If your old thought had a lot of blue in the picture and the new one had a lot of red, then replace the colors. If the old thought has the sound a timid voice in it, and the new one has a picture of a school hall and the sound of the wind outside, then picture your school hall, and hear the words the timid voice was saying as if the wind was saying it. Secondly, it is essential to stay single-minded while making the changes. You must be in a place with no distractions and you must close your eyes. Some people can do this technique while shopping in a supermarket but learners generally need lots of focus. Lastly, you can make the changes stick by making changes on the outside. Imagine that you change the thought of not having enough money to the thought of having plenty of money. If you do not allow that thought to change your actual spending, or the way you interact in your working relationships, then it is not as likely to stick. Likewise, if you change a thought of low self-worth to one of power and accomplishment, then you must actually allow that change to alter the tone of your voice and your body posture. Remember, that an inner transformation is worth nothing to you if you can't see it on the outside. So, in summary, be specific in your characteristics, focus when you make the change, then back it up with real world actions.

Personal Story

HECTOR is a scatterbrain. I am sure he won't mind me calling him that as he also has a great sense of humor. He simply finds it hard to focus on the issues that are really important in his life. When he called me to make an appointment, it was evident that he was unsure exactly what he needed to do to be happier with his life. During our first meeting, it transpired that he had always felt lonely. Having grown up in Norway as an immigrant with no brothers or sisters, he had many outside factors with which to tell himself he was lonely. I asked him how he knew that he was lonely. He told me that he had always thought of himself as such. I asked him if he had ever considered that maybe he wasn't lonely any more but that the thought from the past continued to tell him to have a lonely feeling. He told me he had never considered this. So, I set to work to find out exactly how he constructed his "I'm lonely" thoughts. I asked him to think of a specific time in his life when he was especially lonely, one that was a particularly good example of what he was describing. He closed his eyes and remembered a memory from the past. He told me that when he was at college five years previously, he had been with a girlfriend that he really loved. At that time he wanted to marry her. He remembered not having the courage to ask her to marry him. Their relationship deteriorated rapidly after that point. While he was deep in the memory, I asked him to focus on the way he was thinking. He told me he could hear a firm, serious voice inside his head saying, "You'll always be alone. Don't even bother asking her to marry you." Next, I asked him to think of a time when he felt liked he belonged, like he was totally together with other people. He remembered a time when he was on drugs and felt totally connected to the group of people he was with. It was obviously not healthy for him to rely on drugs for these feelings, but I knew that once a person has a feeling they can recreate it all by themselves. I got him to remember the experience vividly, and tell me about how he was thinking. He told me he just remembered physical warmth toward them. I asked him again how he thought towards them. He told me that his mind kept shouting "Yippee! Yippee!" in an excited voice. Next, I asked him to remember the girlfriend experience again and to change the voice so it shouted, "You'll always be alone. Don't even bother asking her to marry you," in a loud excited voice. This was using the content from the old thought and the characteristic of the new empowering thought. Then I asked him how to imagine a social interaction in the future and to check how he felt about it. He did this and told me he felt very connected. I asked him to go and seek social situations that week and to enjoy the new feelings and the ways of thinking that supported them. Three months later he was in another relationship and had grown his group of friends. He told me, "I feel so happy, like I belong now." His unconscious had simply been shown a new way to think, which then produced new feelings.

9

EMPOWER YOUR BODY

"He who has health has hope, and he who has hope has everything."
Arabian Proverb

"The higher your energy level, the more efficient your body. The more efficient your body, the better you feel and the more you will use your talent to produce outstanding results."
Anthony Robbins

"The secret of health for both mind and body is not to mourn for the past, worry about the future, or anticipate troubles, but to live in the present moment wisely and earnestly."
Buddha

"And forget not that the earth delights to feel your bare feet and the winds long to play with your hair."
Kahlil Gibran

Know It Inside Out

THE body is the crucible of God. It is the most tangible part of you that expresses God in the world. You absolutely rely on the body in order to exist. The body holds the lowest vibration of all the vehicles, with the mind having the highest and the emotions in the middle. This means that while the mind can move fast and change quickly, the emotions move more slowly and so change more slowly. Meanwhile, the body moves even more slowly than that, so produces the slowest rate of change. This is why the body must be nurtured on an on-going basis. Instant results, while possible, cannot be expected. Some results only manifest in the body after years of repeated behavior. Making a temporary change has little effect on the body. If you want to change your fitness, strength, resistance to disease and overall health, you must make and maintain a complete upgrade of your lifestyle.

The Human body is very complex and has yet to be fully understood by anyone. However, we do know that the body will do the best it can to produce health and power wherever possible. Physical power is only limited by unnatural constraints put upon it, for example a sedentary lifestyle, a careless injury or a diet of processed food. The body will always do the best it can.

To understand your own body, you can increase your sensitivity to it by opening up your awareness to it. This means that you cease, once and for all, to close off the signals of pain that the body gives off. Everyone is very open to signals of pleasure from the body but the typical response in a modern head-oriented society is to close off from any painful signals. This means that there must be a disconnection between the body and consciousness so that pain can be avoided. Of course, the pain is really still there, but if you know how to cut it off then you can numb yourself from the experience of it. Painkillers, alcohol, and TV are typically used for this purpose. Ironically, the result of cutting off from the body's pain is that you inadvertently cut off from its pleasure too. In short, you get completely cut off from it. Most people in the modern world exist *outside of their body*. They use the body like a tool to maneuver around the planet in search of a release from the pain that is being held in the body. However, beyond this there is little or no contact with the body so the pain stays unconscious. In such a state people can do the most incredible things, for example breathing in highly toxic fumes in the name of smoking, overworking to the point of disease, and swallowing pharmaceuticals just because someone who has never actually tried them for themselves says it is the best thing. The result is a climate of major discontent and separation from the body. Of course, separation from the body is the first point of separation from all material things. When we get more and more distant from the world around us, we begin to need greater and greater stimuli in order to feel grounded and therefore more alive. Hence the popularity of addictions like computer games, pornography, alcohol, loud music, and shopping. These provide such intensity that for a moment contact is regained with the body and sanity is temporarily restored. However, the cost of addictive behavior is unnecessary wear and tear on the body.

To remedy this disconnection we must exist in our body and feel the pleasure *and* the pain within it. Only then can we move forward without the fear of unconscious pain driving us into further ill health. We all have the power to do this, so why don't we?

THE ROAD TO SEPARATION

WE are taught from a young age that pleasure is good and pain is bad. There is some value in this since it is obvious that playing on a swing is good while cutting oneself on barbed wire is bad. The body will naturally move towards pleasure and away from pain, in every given circumstance except where to move towards pain will eventually result in even greater pleasure. Because of this natural movement, we do not need to put a value of good on pleasure and bad on pain. Rather we need to learn the strategies for avoiding pain and moving towards pleasure. It is the lack of these strategies that lead people to sever consciousness from their bodies. When you know how to deal with pain in a mature and sophisticated way, you need not run from it, hide from it or try to escape from it. You can face it, hear its message and take the action that sets the pain free. Forever.

The first step is to recognize that moral values of pain and pleasure are not useful and that we need to improve our strategies of dealing with pain. This then gives us the power and courage to listen to our body and make the necessary adjustments to set the pain free so that it never comes back. Pain is simply a message that tells us we are doing something that is not in keeping with the natural flow of God. We must therefore come back into that flow before the pain will vanish.

A common example is back pain. The back will tell a person that they must change the way they do things because it is not in keeping with the natural flow of God within them. In other words, what they are doing is not congruent with showing love to themselves. The way the back tells a person this is by sending a message of pain. That message can either be ignored or acted upon. However it can only be acted upon if you know what to do. So often people are bereft of knowledge, understanding and intuition about their own bodies, that they will ignore the pain and instead seek a temporary escape from it. This results in severing consciousness from the body's pleasure and pain. The alternative route is seeking a practitioner that can relieve us from our own ignorance of our body's needs. The problem with this is that the vast majority of health professionals do not actually know what your body needs because they fail to enquire as to your specific history and needs. Therefore, by going to a modern health practitioner you are very likely to get someone who needs clients like you to keep their profession in work. They will likely give you a treatment that suppresses the message of the pain. However, there are some effective health practitioners out there and I wish you luck in finding one. A good benchmark to use is long-term results, since most practitioners can do something that will ease the pain short term.

The only way forward out of the quagmire of disease and half cures is to become responsible for the way you use your body and to learn the strategies for improving health so that the pain leaves. This means that when we get a message of pain, it provides us with an opportunity to improve our physical health. Pain that is left untreated will continue to get louder and louder in the body, moving to new places and new depths within the body to get its message across. If we do not respond to it at all, the ultimate result is death from a fatal illness. The majority of people in the western world are going to experience this. Are you going to be one of them? Or are you going to commit some time, energy and money to learning what your body needs and how to give it that?

It amazes me how low the body has become on the western man's list of priorities. People will cut the cost of their food shopping in order to smoke and drink, or they will fail to take sufficient breaks from stressful work. The result is a whole lot of people leading disgruntled lives without actually being able to put their finger on why they feel the way they do. The only healers around them are often doctors that are offered attractive financial bonuses to ensure that you end up with a particular brand of drug. The time is now to get a hold of your physical health. Remember that your job and your family, your house, and your car, will not be there for you if you are not there for your body. A tiny bit of illness is usually enough to remind someone how important the body is to them, yet it is amazing how once the illness is suppressed, the person can then carry on without even remembering being ill. This is an indication of severance between consciousness and the body.

So where do we learn what our body needs, and how to give to it? Well, this chapter is by no means the last word on this topic, but it can open doors for you. I suggest you read up thoroughly on nutrition, exercise and breathing. Then, of course, do the techniques that seem best for you. Learn from those who are exhibiting high levels of health, strength, fitness and resistance to disease. Find out what they do. But more than anything, listen to your body.

Eating for Health

ONCE you read four or five nutrition books it will become evident that there is conflicting advice in all of them. So rather than defining any one system, what nutritional research can do is open up your behavioral options. This means that you can try eating different things, or supplementing your food with oils, vitamins or minerals to determine the effects of doing that. The information in this chapter is no substitute for an integrated nutrition program delivered by a professional. Since your body is unique, there is no way that I can know what you need, however there are some general conclusions that we can make.

To keep it simple, there are four basic essential nutrients we need in our diet: water, fat, carbohydrate and protein. Without any one of these we are going to experience major problems. Minerals and vitamins are also important, but as we shall see, if you eat well you can get most of these from the carbohydrate group.

1. The need to remove dehydration

When the body is starved of water, it creates great upset throughout the body. Nutrients cannot be passed around effectively and cell communication is interrupted. To remove dehydration, a good starting can be to drink water. A good amount to drink is between 4 and 8 pints of pure, body temperature water. Other drinks such as teas, coffee, juices or sodas do not count towards this amount. Water is useful in removing dehydration but it will do very little if that water is simply passed out the other end. To hold the water in place, we need the right kind of oils in our diet.

2. Fat is essential

Even with all the conflicting advice in modern nutrition, one thing remains fairly consistent, and that is that certain types of fat are essential to our diet. One of the major roles that fat plays in the body is to build cell walls. It is through these cell walls that cells communicate and pass substances to one another. So much of our physical health depends on the health of our cells because we are, after all, a mass of them. If our cells communicate well, then we can communicate well with our body and also with other people. Essential Fatty Acids (or EFAs) are the type of fats that are essential to good cell wall design. They allow for greater cell health and improved communication. The EFAs that are most useful to us are known as Omega-3 and Omega-6. While there is some controversy over optimum daily dosages, current research shows that more Omega-3 than Omega-6 is necessary. A great source of these EFAs is found in fish oil. Another good source is flax oil. This can be consumed daily for improved resistance to disease, better focus and a more stable metabolism. You may find that the body needs help in absorbing the oils so lecithin, an emulsifier, can be consumed along with the oils to aid this. Oils hold water in the body thereby assisting in hydration. The daily combination of five pints of pure water, two grams of fish oil, and a teaspoon of lecithin could set you on your way to greater health and longevity.

3. Eating the Greens

The modern diet is usually lacking in the green vegetables. It is these vegetables that give us quality carbohydrates and a rich supply of vitamins and minerals. Eating plenty of these vegetables will supply you with carbohydrates, from which the body produces energy. Prepare these at home for the best effect, and avoid processed or tinned versions. The best quality is always fresh local organic produce and it is always worth the extra effort and money to get hold of them. In warm weather, eating vegetables raw in a salad is great, while in a cold weather, steaming and sweating the vegetables is the best way of preserving their precious vitamins and minerals. Steaming is easily done using a saucepan and steaming basket, while sweating is a lovely way to cook. Simply melt a knob of butter in a saucepan on a very low heat, and put on the lid. Cut the vegetables starting with the slowest cooking ones. As soon as a vegetable is cut, tip it into the pan and replace the lid. Stir every few minutes. What will happen is that the vegetables start to release their own juices and cook themselves gently in them.

4. The body builder

Proteins repair the body and so are essential for anyone that wants to do more exercise than simply sitting on an office chair. There are a number of essential amino acids that need to be consumed on a regular basis. Good sources of protein include meat, fish, dairy, pulses and nuts. Again, as with all these recommendations, eat according to the true signals within your body.

5. MOVE THAT BODY!

SOMETIMES, you just have to do something new in order to break an old habit. Regular exercise can take the form of moving around more during the day or taking part in some kind of structured exercise like running or swimming. If you do not already exercise, then now is the time to start. Regular active use of the body means that your body will be there when you need it. Exercise oxygenates the blood, increases blood flow, releases toxins via the lymph system and strengthens muscle tissue.

It is ironic that when people defend themselves in my seminars about their lack of energetic movement, they often say that they are too tired to exercise after a long day at work. However, when I ask I usually find out that this long working day is less than eight hours, and that in fact they are tired because they did so little physical activity that day! The body is an habitual creature and will prepare itself to do more of whatever you are doing with it right now. If you oversleep, the body will feel sleepy. If you sit around all day, your body will feel like sitting around some more. To break that cycle, get up and move! Swimming, dancing, walking and love-making are all excellent natural exercises that get the heart pumping, and set the blood and the lymph flowing. The following simple exercise can help you to strengthen your body, giving you easier emotional expression, enhanced self-esteem and greater physical health.

Exercise

Write down parts of your body that you wish to improve. Decide whether you want to strengthen, tone, heal, build muscle in or increase flexibility in them.

Write down for each body part how you are going to achieve that. Give yourself a schedule that is easy to achieve so that you are confident that you will do it.

Give yourself time in which to help your body and devote energy to achieving the above task. Start doing it, and continue until you have achieved what you set out to do.

Sleepy Head?

DO you sleep all night without waking once, even to go to the toilet? If you do, then you know how blissful sound sleep is. If not, then please find solace in the knowledge that you can. The way most people I know sleep is they sleep *for the mind*. What I mean by this is that they use their mind more than their body during the day so their mind requires more rest than their body does. Therefore they are used to doing things with and for the mind, while the body takes second place. As a result of great importance being placed on the mind, the length of sleep is then dictated by mental tiredness. People that sleep eight or nine hours a night commonly have a very active mental day and a very inactive physical day. Rebalancing this imbalance can begin with getting your sleep right. Six to seven hours of unbroken sleep is optimal. Try the following exercise to connect more with your body and combat sluggishness. If you try this exercise for two weeks, you will probably notice a big difference in the quality of sleep you get. Your body is likely to become more active, while your mind will become a little slower. This may mean you can get more things done, without thinking too much about them.

Exercise

In the evening, go to bed when you start yawning.

In the morning, get up as soon as you wake up. You can go back to sleep if the sky is pitch black. Otherwise, do not go back to sleep. Get up even if you have been woken by a noise or by the need to urinate.

Stay up for the rest of the day.

If you feel excessively tired or start yawning during the day, then take a nap of less then one hour. If you are not able to do this because of daytime commitments then get an early night.

Breathe In, Breathe Out

BREATHING is also a key to good physical health. The breath is your body's direct connection to God. There is nothing like the breath to make you aware of the undeniable fact that there is a force flowing through you. Even if you cease to do any activity whatsoever, the breath will continue to flow. This is the very life force of love. It nurtures the body and benevolently gives life to it. This love is God flowing into form. We exist only because of this flow. The breath is not the only form of this flow but it is the one that is most easily contacted. Whenever I find someone who is distressed, worried, anxious or panicky, they always exhibit irregular or forced breathing patterns. It is often accompanied by over-breathing, under-breathing or interrupted breaths. Conversely, when I encounter a relaxed, empowered individual they always breathe in a deep, regular, rhythmic and open way. See the effect that breathing has on your emotional state by trying the following exercise:

EXERCISE

Start by taking overly deep breaths quickly. How does that make you feel?

Next, try breathing slow shallow breaths. How does this feel?

Finally breathe deeply yet slowly into your belly. Again, notice how breathing patterns affect your emotional state.

Next, let the breath come and go without any control by you. Do this for about five minutes. You can close your eyes, and simply allow the breath to breathe all by itself. Notice the power that makes the breath flow. What is it like? How do you relate to it? How do you feel about it?

QUESTIONS AND ANSWERS

Q: I have tried changing my sleep patterns and now get up as soon as I wake up. I feel alive and awake all day until the evening. I like to exercise in the evening as it is the only time I have free to do it during my working week. However, I usually do not have the energy to go to my health club for a workout. How can I get more energy?

A: If you come home physically tired after a day at the office, it is because you are not doing enough physical activity during the day. Remember the body will prepare to do more of what you have already done with it. It will expect that, because you have been sedentary all day, you will continue like that into the evening. You simply have to break the pattern consciously by making effort to be a little more active during your working day. Perhaps take a walk at lunchtime and get some daylight, whatever the weather. Next, you can break the pattern of not exercising by beginning to exercise even when if feel tired. It is very likely that if you do this, you will feel uplifted and liberated. Next time, the association of exercising after work will be a good one, so it will become easier. Over time, you can either consider switching to a more active job, or find ways in your current one to be even more active. For example, you can take regular walks across the office and makes stretches often. Swimming before work may also be a help. Most importantly, find a form of exercise that you sincerely enjoy as this will keep you focused and interested in it. Do some form of exercise three times a week for about half and hour at a time. Then work your way up to five times a week for up to an hour. Remember it is regularity that counts. Little and often is great!

Q: I want to build up a meaningful relationship with my body, but whenever I get in touch with it, I feel overwhelming pain. I cannot bear to feel this, so I retract from my body and numb it or forget about it. How can I get over this?

A: What you talk about is very common. Because of the mental teaching that pain is "bad", we have devised strategies for ignoring pain by suppressing it. This is very dangerous. Pain is a message that we have done something that is not wholesome for us. Therefore the pain is telling us that this way of doing things needs to change if health is to be maintained. If this message is not heard and respected, it becomes louder and louder in order to get its point across. At its loudest, pain manifests as a full-blown disease. Pain is vital to health because when you are able to feel pain in the body, you are able to understand its message, and subsequently take action to release that pain forever. The reluctance of people to feel pain in the body stems from a fear of the body's natural wisdom. Technological societies have become so disconnected with the natural rhythms of the world, of seasons and lunar or solar cycles, that people have become detached from their own bodies. The only way that we can live in full health is to embrace pain within the body, then own it, and finally take responsibility for its release. This can mean learning from others what part of the body the pain is in, what that body part is for, why the pain might have arisen, and how to set it free. This is such a liberating process as it puts you back in the body. Because of the reluctance to feel pain, there is a lot of pain in your body right now. It has been building up over years, waiting to be heard and understood. Now you have made the commitment to feeling your body, the first layer of sensation you have to deal with is the most urgent one to turn your attention to. It is pain. Allow yourself to feel the pain, become smaller than the pain and go inside it. Here you can find out where the pain is, and perhaps why it got to be there. If you cannot do this, seek help from someone who can assist you. But, remember, take responsibility. You created that pain through your actions and your heritage. You have the power to unlock it and release it forever. The results are so worthwhile, because once you can hear the message of pain in the body, you can also hear the message of pleasure.

Personal Story

DAVINA was a fifty-something woman who was overweight. She came to me for the simple physical reason of weight loss. She also had issues around lack of money and was out of work. In short, they were both issues about control. There was a lack of control over her weight and her finances. When I enquired as to her weight in the past, she told me that twenty years earlier, just after she was married, she was also overweight and had lost plenty of weight in a short period of time. I asked her what was going on at that time. She told me that she simply decided to lose weight and began to eat more vegetables and fish, and fewer sweets. She lost five stone in just five months. She used to buy a Mars Bar from the local shop, bite the top of it, and throw it over her shoulder for a passing dog to gobble up. She did this every day as a symbol of her power to control her diet. I then asked her what her diet was like, and found it was heavy in wheat, grains and dairy produce. She agreed to cut out wheat completely, reduce dairy, reduce grains, eat more fish and vegetables, eat more fresh food, and eat two tablespoons of flax every day. She also agreed to open three new bank accounts so that she could start learning how to save. On top of this, I asked her to buy a Mars Bar every day, bite the top off it and discard the rest of it. She not only *did* all of these actions but she also found herself some active work in a rest home.

She called me up ten days after the session in a joyful mood and proclaiming that she had lost ten pounds. She thanked me several times, and sounded jubilant to be back in control of her life. Her body, like everyone's, had become a metaphor for the way she was behaving in the world. She regained control and enjoyed the results of that in her body.

10

EMPOWER YOUR EMOTIONS

"Seeing's believing, but the feeling's the truth."
Thomas Fuller

"Nobody can make you feel inferior without your consent."
Eleanor Roosevelt

"The more often a man feels without acting, the less he'll be able to act. And in the long run, the less he'll be able to feel."
C.S. Lewis

"It's the end of the world as we know it ... and I feel fine."
REM

Feel It All Now!

FEEL your emotions fully! They connect you with the world around you. Cutting off from your emotions is like severing your connection with the world. Every emotion is positive. Unexpressed emotion, however, can have negative consequences. This chapter cleanses you of past emotional worries. The aim of years of therapy can be achieved by you in a few days using simple techniques. You can learn that you recreate a past emotion by making it in the body. When you are conscious of how you do this, you can stop the feeling and become free of the past. Once cleansed, you can relate to the world again with a depth of emotion that is totally related to the present moment. You no longer have to close off to an "unsavory" emotion. You can learn how to be fully angry, sad, happy, excited, fearful, jealous, ecstatic, funny or determined without the expression of those feelings having any negative impact on you or anyone else.

Feeling Great?

THE most common reason that a person will come to me will be about a feeling they have. When a person has a pain in their body, what usually disturbs them the most is how they feel about that pain. If someone is undergoing a major life change, like a divorce or changing jobs, it is the feelings they experience during the change that they most readily talk about. When a person shows up in sheer desperation in their life, they generally feel terrible about things. When someone comes seeking improvement in a life that is already great, they will typically feel uncomfortable about not living to their full potential. From homeless people to millionaires, the people I meet all have areas of their life that they desire to improve or change. And what brings people to that desire? You guessed it: their emotion.

Emotion is the touchstone of our experience. When we desire more physical strength or more financial wealth, it is the feeling it gives us that we truly seek. The power and the money mean very little if having them does not make us feel great to be alive.

The way we feel things can be seen on two levels. Firstly, we get physical sensations in our body that relate to the environment. For example, you can feel the wind on your face, or an upset stomach from eating unwholesome food. But there is another kind of feeling that occurs on a more subtle level. This is an emotion and we can call it an "inner" feeling. Like physical sensation, it relates to the environment and is a cellular reaction to a change. Emotion is created by waves of communication throughout the cells of the body. This cellular communication then becomes a way for us to gauge what a situation means to us. We then get an opportunity to respond to it.

How Emotion Works

JUST like physical sensations, emotion tells us something about who we are and something about the environment we are in. What strikes me as amazing is that, although emotion and physical sensation are very close in character, people will exercise immense amounts of control over physical sensation and very little over emotion. For example, if a person lives in a house that is uncomfortably cold, they will usually turn on the heating. They will even work all day so that they can afford heating in their home. Yet when it comes to an emotion like anger, how many of us actually instigate a change? And how many of us know how to? This chapter will impart powerful tools to change your emotional state when you require it. But first, let's look at why we have emotion and when it may be necessary to change it.

When we feel something, we feel it inside the body. One example is a person walking closely to a cliff edge. They may feel fear as a contraction within their gut. The fear tells them to pay extra attention to their actions. This emotion serves a person very well. Another example is someone who has lost a family member that they adore. They feel grief-stricken. The grief feels like a heavy ball in their chest pulling downwards. This emotion allows that person to let go of their family member. These two examples are examples of "present emotions". In other words, the emotions that they are feeling relate directly to the circumstances of that person's current life. They also serve to put that person in touch with an experience that will enable them to develop and grow as a human being.

However, there are many times, when people report to me that what they are feeling seems to be a present emotion, yet is not beneficial to them. For example someone might feel nervous about a job interview while another may feel sad when it is raining. These situations are obviously very real to that person, but the emotional response to them stems from the past. What can sometimes happen is that we experience an event with a very strong emotional charge attached to it, and then we unconsciously remember how to repeat that feeling in the future. This repetition of a past feeling tends to happen when we are reminded of the original emotional experience. For example, someone may be nervous for a job interview because they felt nervous the very first time they went to school. When an external stimulus reminded them of the original situation then the old feeling gets replayed. This is obvious in phobias, where someone may have had a terrifying experience of a spider at some stage of their life, and from then on they experience every spider in that way. Another example is when a woman once felt about her father in a certain way and that then affects the way she feels about all other men. Likewise men's past emotion towards their mothers can influence their interactions with women. The power of the unconscious to trick us into the same feelings, even though we are in a new situation, can stop us from being "emotionally present". It can grab a hold of us and put us back in the past. However, it is possible to change this unconscious process, using some simple tools. By learning and using these tools you can change any emotion that stems from the past. By doing so, you can become emotionally present and respond to what is around you clearly and intelligently.

An emotion is coming from the past if it does not seem to reflect the "true you". Since emotion is essential to our contact with others and with the world, we do not want to change our present emotions. Past emotions, however, only serve to disconnect us from being our true selves in the present moment. As such, they can be changed with full force and effect to lead to a greater sense of authenticity and connectedness with the present moment.

Exercise

Choose an emotional state that seems to plague you. Make sure it is one that you would truly love to change, and start with one that is relatively mild. You can use this technique on any depth of emotion once you know how, but starting with a mild one is good for now.

Close your eyes and breathe three deep breaths in and out. Connect with your body.

Imagine a time when you strongly felt the emotion you wish to change. See where you were, hear what was going on, and feel fully that emotion in your body.

Locate the emotion and write down exactly where in the body the feeling is.

Next, detect the movement of the feeling. Is it circling, spiraling, tingling, swinging, expanding, contracting, moving backwards, forwards, upwards, downwards, outwards, inwards, or some other kind of movement? Write down the way the emotion moves inside your body.

Then, describe the feeling to yourself in terms of real-world objects and real-world physics. For example, you might describe it as being like a cold, clenched fist, or a heavy stone swinging like a pendulum. Write down this description.

Now, think of a new experience where you felt utterly empowered and alive. Choose one where you felt intense feelings of happiness, courage, power, satisfaction, contentment, or whatever you would like to feel in place of the unwanted emotion.

Again, find out where the feeling is, how it moves and what it resembles in the real physical world. Write this information down so that you have the location, movement and description of the feeling you want of change *and* the new feeling you would like in its place.

Tell yourself out loud that you are going to teach your unconscious something that you want it to understand and use so that it can produce the new feeling whenever you need it.

Next, go back to the first emotion – the one you want to change. Again close your eyes, and put yourself back there so that you can see, hear and feel what is happening there.

Now, change the direction of this emotion by changing it to the direction of the desired emotion. For example if it is moving downwards, and the desired emotion is moving upwards and outwards, then change the direction from downwards to upwards and outwards. By the way, you *can* do this simply because it was you who created the emotion in the first place. You therefore have the power to change it further.

Next, change the physical resemblance to that of the desired emotion. For example if the first emotion was a closed fist, and the second one was a fountain, visualize and feel the fist opening and imagine it turning to water and spraying upwards. If you have ever seen film special effects, you know this is possible.

Now, change the location of this feeling to the location of the desired emotion.

Open your eyes, and finally, check the effectiveness of this process by imagining a scenario in the future. Close your eyes. Imagine a situation in the future that might have caused you to feel the old emotion. Put yourself into that scenario by imagining what it would look like, and sound like. Imagine what you would be doing and how you would behave. Notice how you feel. Is it different? Is it radically improved? If so, the process was a success.

Watch how different you are in the world next time this kind of situation happens to you. Enjoy the empowering emotion you feel!

QUESTIONS AND ANSWERS

Q: I find it almost impossible to quantify my emotion. I just feel it. I have never tried to analyze what it is, or why it is there. But I do know that I want to feel differently at times. How can I best identify my emotion?

A: Every emotion that we feel is felt in the body. Therefore, you do not need to analyze your feelings so much as connect to them through the body. When you become more and more aware of how your emotion moves in your body, then you will be able to exercise control by changing old, outdated emotions. One thing that can help this greatly is to sit down in a quiet place, and close your eyes. Next, visualize the scariest event of your entire life. Pay close attention to what happens to your body. Notice any feelings that are present. You must have feeling present if you are remembering vividly a very scary experience. Talk out loud to yourself about the feelings. As you do this, do not try to grasp what is happening. Just let your voice make identifications for you. For example, "I am breathing a little more heavily. I feel faint. I feel light-headed. I feel like my stomach is burning." These are all clear indicators of your emotional flow. Next, visualize a time when you felt very confident and powerful. Again, let your voice talk for you to identify the exact feelings. You now have indictors for both emotional states. Simply perform the switch as described in this chapter and enjoy the results!

Q: I have a feeling that I cannot change using this method. I have tried five times now to shift it but to no avail. Am I doing something wrong?

A: No, you have followed the instructions accurately. The emotion you are trying to change is lodged very deeply in the unconscious. In other words, the way it plays itself out seems to be very involuntary, as if it is compulsive. What you need to do therefore, to effect a change, is to connect with your unconscious on a deeper level before you start the transfer of location, movement and description. To do this, you can spend five or ten minutes just breathing. Breathe deeply at first then just let the breath breathe all by itself. Notice the rise and fall of your chest, and let any thoughts come and go. If you get distracted by anything, bring your attention to your hands, where you will normally feel a tingling sensation. During this exercise, you can relax. You will notice how becoming aware of the breath will relax you, as will letting thoughts come and go. Any tingling in the hands can further add to that sense of peace and calm. When you feel gently relaxed and focused, then you can carry out the exercise. In this way, you have first contacted a 'deeper' level of unconscious functioning and the change should be easier to effect.

PERSONAL STORY

A client of mine, Jacqui, told me that she is terrified of public speaking. She would get up in front of a crowd and literally begin to shake. Her heart rate would go up, she would sweat profusely, and her voice would stammer and waver. To change this kind of emotional response, it is not necessary to know the cause of it, but in this example I will show you. I asked her what her first experiences of public speaking were. She told me that ever since school she had always hated speaking in groups. She said it made her feel shy and uncomfortable. I asked her to close her eyes and to relax which she did. After suggesting she connect to her breath for a few minutes, I asked her to think of her very first memory of being shy and uncomfortable while talking in a group. Jacqui opened her eyes and told me with a startled look that she recalled a time at school when a teacher she detested and feared asked her to get up and read to the rest of the class. When she stumbled over a word, the teacher sternly corrected her. She became more nervous, and got more and more words wrong. Her first public speaking experience ended with the teacher telling her to sit down while a more capable child read instead. With this emotional response fully installed, her unconscious repeated it every time she was required to talk in public. There is no clear indication of why some emotions get repeated unconsciously and some do not, but the intensity of the emotional charge certainly appears to be factor. So Jacqui replayed those emotions again and again since that incident. I asked her how it felt, and she told me that she had a spinning feeling in her abdomen. The cells were communicating to each other in a clockwise circle. She described it as "a very fast washing machine." I asked her for an emotion she would rather feel which she said would be "elation." I asked her to remember a time when she was elated. She remembered a time when she won an athletics race at school and was awarded a trophy for it. She felt wonderful and described this as an elated feeling that "shimmered like water" all over her body. I explained to her that although she did not need to relax, she could *relax* as much as she wished. I then asked her to close her eyes and imagine herself getting up to give a talk to a group. She got visibly uncomfortable at this thought. I then gently suggested that she slow down the clockwise spinning in her abdomen and eventually bring it to a stop. Next, I suggested that she produce the shimmering feelings all over her body. Her face lit up, and she began to smile.

Two months after that session I spoke to Jacqui about her progress. I was delighted to hear that she had given four formal presentations in the last month as part of her job and that she had no problems with any of them.

PART 4

GUIDE YOURSELF

In this final part of the book, we will explore the way in which you can design a life that you truly love. Imagine what your life would be like if there were no limitations on what you could achieve or who you could become. Life would become a reflection of your heart's desires and you would therefore be surrounded by the fruits of your loving action. This is the only way to be fulfilled during this lifetime, so let's learn how.

11

Guide to Your Heart

"Love, not reason should make your decisions."
Adi Da Samraj

"In spite of everything, I still believe that people are really good at heart."
Anne Frank

"It is only with the heart that one can see rightly. What is essential is invisible to the eye."
Antoine de Saint-Exupery

"Come away with me through the fields, and we will be careless and happy, and we will leave thought to find us when it can, for that is the duty of thought, and it is more anxious to find us than we are to be found."
James Stephens

WHERE ARE YOU GOING?

IF you do not know where you are going, it is unlikely you will get there! In order to get to a place of fulfillment, peace and satisfaction in your life, it is essential to identify what that place would look like and feel like. If you know where you are heading, you infinitely increase your chances of arriving there. Randomly moving around in the world according to the whims of others is not a good idea. You will become a puppet of the media and of the people around you. You will forfeit your personal sovereignty in favor of being told what to do. It is now time to connect with your heart and discover exactly what you want your life to be all about. The previous chapters showed what you are, and how to know yourself more intimately. This chapter empowers you with a vision born of your own heart. You can use this vision to steer a course through life that is truly unique, that is truly yours.

A vision born of your love will bear fruits that are a reflection of your own inner love.

When you do something from your heart, not only is the vision part of your heart, but the results you get are as well. That means that any fruits of your actions are your inner heart in external form. If you build a job or relationship based on your true heart's desire, then that job or relationship will be your heart expressed in the external world. When your heart spills out around you in this way, your experience of life will be that the world around you is the very same as your heart. Your experience of the world will be that it is *made of love*.

This makes life a wondrous playground where love is experienced in every moment in the external world. This grounds what you are as God in the world and allows the full expression of God to flow through your heart and out into actions and objects.

The path of the heart will make you appreciate how whole you really are as you see that this love is the God within you expressing itself in the world. When you apply your heart to your actions then all areas of life become more satisfying. When you earn money, you are better able to use it to buy something you really love; when you are in a relationship, you are better able to show love to your partner through specific actions; when you work in a job, you are better able to perform at a peak level because of a natural passion born of love. Simply put, you will begin to fly in all areas of your life.

Making Huge Improvements Can Be Simple

FOLLOWING your heart usually means making big changes in your life. You may discover that making huge changes in your personal life is actually very simple. All it requires are the following values: a commitment to your truth, courage to take action, and persistence if changes do not happen instantly.

Commitment to your truth means that you hold what is true for you high in your value system. Note that I say "your truth". This is because truth is very personal. The One Truth is synonymous with the Universe, God or the Tao. The One Truth manifests itself in many different ways depending on an individual's perception. No one can know the whole of the One Truth, yet everyone is a living representative of it. The way everyone describes the One Truth is totally different, and it is therefore their own personal truth.

Once you have become aware of your truth and you decide to hold it high in your value system, you have to find the courage to put it into action. This means taking the risk of change. Change is always risky because it involves a step into the unknown. To take this step confidently takes the faith that following your own truth is the best thing for you. This faith in your path is called courage. The courage to transform your life for the better is one of the most challenging parts of personal development because it involves moving through fear. New changes are usually accompanied by a little bit of fear. Change can mean leaving the comfort zone of familiarity and entering the unknown. Such a change takes a great leap of faith.

The final factor that guarantees success is persistence. The persistence to continue following your truth in the face of adversity is what separates you from falling into denial and rising into success. If you follow your heart, you will find that your direction is defined by you, not by what the world allows to work for you. If in your heart you know the direction of your life, then persistence is the mechanism that will ensure you get there. Giving up as soon as the world does not fit your criteria could mean sacrificing your heart's path simply because you cannot see your own possibilities of success.

Persistence brings results. Persistence is in itself a measure of success. If you look at the lives of successful people, you will quickly find out that they continued to do what they were doing even when to do so was against all odds. They carried on even when the chips were down and when others were suggesting that their path was too difficult or too ambitious. Persistence is what separates the winners in life from the quitters of life.

When you know in your heart what changes to your life will be truly beneficial for you then persistence will *make it happen*. If you persist at an activity, your talent in it will grow. You will become accomplished at it. You can earn a living from it. You can become famous for it. Persistence is the drive to get what you want. It comes from having a doubtless belief that you will accomplish whatever you set out to do in life.

REAL SUCCESS

SUCCESS can be measured in terms of career, relationships, income, family, status, possessions or fame. However, real success does not come from these outer achievements but rather from honoring your heart as you follow it towards outer achievements. If you honor your heart and follow its guidance, then you will experience success no matter how rich or famous you are and no matter how many friends and family you have. When your heart and your mind aligns, you will find that whatever you accomplish in your life is satisfying. It satisfies you at a heart level because that is where the motivation to achieve your accomplishments was born. When your heart is drawn to achieve something, you will find that achievement to be immensely fulfilling.

Watch out for any pressures on you that tell you not to follow your heart. These pressures are built up by people and systems that are alienated from their hearts' desires. They therefore believe that it is not fair or correct for others to follow their hearts. It is essential that you persist with your heart's path amidst such pressure. The rewards are well worth it.

Until you tune in to your heart's passions, you will always live the lives of your parents. To live your own unique life, you must break out of any restrictive family patterns by following your heart. When you are guided by your heart, things in life are *very* different. Your emotions will flow fully. Your capacity to hold an emotional space will grow. Your mind will become a help, not a hindrance. Your body will become stronger, fitter and healthier. Your relationships will be imbued with trust, respect, honor and integrity. Your work will fill you with warmth and joy. Life will be richer and more exquisite. Pain will be accepted. Pleasure will be enjoyed. It is the biggest revolution that can happen to a person.

Using the following exercise, your heart's path will become clearer to you, and you will begin to explore ways of bringing it about as a reality.

Exercise

Close your eyes and begin to think of all the things that you love. Remember those special places and special times where you felt loved and you felt loving.

Now that you have a connection to the flow of love in your life, write a list of all the things you would love to do, love to be and love to have during your lifetime. At this stage, do not limit yourself. Imagine what you could do, be or have if there was no limitation to your finances or skills.

Next, go through the list and put a tick next to the things that really excite you and that you would really love to do, be or have in your life.

Now write a short story about your life where you are doing, being or having these things. Write it in the present tense, so that you get a feel for what it is really like to be there.

Next, read the story aloud to yourself.

Then close your eyes, and get a sense of what your life will look like at that stage. Get a sense of the people and things that surround you, the way you move, the way you talk, the way you do things, how you feel, what you can hear, what you enjoy most about that way of living.

Next, go through the story and pick out each thing you wish to do, be or have and write down a first step toward accomplishing it. For example, the first step towards accomplishing a career as a football manager may be to call your local Football Association to gather information.

Now you should have a list of first steps that will set you off on a journey towards your heart's path.

Finally, do each of these steps. Just before you do each step, close your eyes again and transport yourself to the scene. Recreate the feeling of being in that place with everything you love around you. Then carry out the action.

Questions and Answers

Q: I want to manifest a life I really, truly love. However I cannot understand how, by doing one step, I am really going to bring this about. I get a sense that it will help me but do not understand how, and therefore find it difficult to get started. Can you explain this exercise in more detail?

A: It is worth mentioning that I have seen this exercise work for many, many people. It is something that really does bring about the magic of a life you really love. The reason that one step can set things in motion is that it is the hardest step to take. Once you set sail in a certain direction, momentum often takes you to your desired end point. But if you never leave port, you can guarantee that you will never get there. The key to this exercise is that you are programming the action with the sense that you have already reached your desired end point. I call this end point your End State since it is about what you have accomplished when you get there *and* how you feel and who you have become during the journey. If I break this exercise down into four steps, it should become clearer for you.

The first step is called Centering. This is where you center your energy on your heart so that you can tune into what you really love in life. This ensures that any life you design for yourself will be one that you love. If you design a life from your mind, you may manifest an intellectually stimulating life, but not one that is truly fulfilling.

The second step is Intention. This is where you actually define what your new life will be like. You write the story in the present tense.

Thirdly, is the End State. Here you put yourself in the story as if you are experiencing it right now, as if it has manifest already. It is this step that tunes you in to the actual eventuality of it, and gives you a sense of its inevitability. You get to feel and see what it is really like at that stage. You also get a sense of who you have become to get there.

Finally, the fourth step is Action. Of course, this is essential because without action nothing gets done. When you act and you put yourself in the End State just before you act, then you are telling yourself that you have already arrived at the place you are heading. What this does is something very mysterious but very practical: it makes the action full of massive confidence where you know the End State is going to happen. This is a source of massive power and can create huge transformations in your life that in turn create huge benefits for you and those around you.

Q: I have great difficulty distinguishing my thoughts from what my heart is telling me. According to you, if I choose a life based on my thoughts, then it is unlikely to satisfy me in any deep way. I want to get this right, but I feel under pressure as a result and cannot readily tune it to what I love. How can I do this?

A: I have said that remembering things and times that you were loved and felt loving will provide a connection to the heart. This is a route to the heart though the mind. You can think of these things and the result can be that thought becomes still and your own heart can show you in words and/or pictures what it would love you to do with your life. You do not have to put yourself under pressure. Many people get confused and inadvertently end up following their thoughts. At least they will have an interesting life from the viewpoint of the mind!

If a person's mind and heart are aligned, then the thoughts will naturally reflect the desires of the heart. However, for anyone who has come from a lifetime of thought-directed action, a rebalancing will need to take place. This means that your heart is given back its natural sovereignty over your personal life. To do this can take a little practice and to make it slightly easier you can do the following. Each time you feel you want to connect with your heart but cannot, take your awareness to the middle of your chest. This is the part of the body that is in closest contact with your inner heart. You can put your hand there if it helps you. Then you can use your mind to focus your awareness on the heart by asking what you love in the present situation. If you have any thoughts that distract you, make sure that you love them. This channels your awareness to the heart. Whenever you consciously love something in the present moment, you are connecting to the heart. Once you have your attention trained there, you will find that your awareness will naturally go to the heart whenever you are curious to know what it is you love right now. Then the heart can guide you in designing the life you would love the most.

Personal Story

GEORGIO is an English man born of Italian parentage. When I met him, he had recently left a high-flying job with one of the world's major marketing companies. His specialty was branding and he worked on many of the world's largest brands. You will be familiar with many of them, and his work is likely to be in your house right now on the side of a food package. He told me how he got tired of the work he was doing and without really knowing why, he dropped out of his job. He moved away from London where he was living and moved back to live with his parents on the south coast of England. Then he hit a major low in his life. He knew he did not want to continue peddling the rat race with major corporations but was confused as to why that was.

When he came to me, we had to get things in perspective. Since he was prone to worry, I encouraged him to quit thinking so much about what he had done and to go deeper into himself for the answer. Using memories of loving times, he was able to connect with his heart and from that space I asked him why he had left his job in London. He replied with utmost clarity, "I didn't love what I had become in order to be successful in that industry." I then asked him to write down precisely what he did love, and to construct a new life story from that list. He did this and found that he was pleasantly surprised. He discovered that he wanted to be a teacher so that he could give others the skills he had, to find a partner, to pay off his debts, and to settle down in his own home. To his ears, his story sounded like it was a million miles away, even though I had him imagining it within three years. So to connect him to the End State of living that life, I asked him to close his eyes and imagine himself to be there already. He did this and smiled. He told me how wonderful he felt. As he was still there, I asked him to imagine talking to the self that was sitting in front of me. He did this, and started up an out-loud conversation between his present self and his future self. His future self was actually instructing his present self as to how to get into the state he was in. He told his present self what his first steps needed to be. When he opened his eyes again, he wrote down all the information his future self had given him.

I saw him two years later, and he had carried out about three quarters of the tasks that he had been given that day. In my experience as long as the majority of tasks are completed, then the majority of the new life will become manifest. When I saw him, he confidently told me how he was now a full-time lecturer with a prestigious university and that he had met a beautiful woman. He had decided that instead of paying off his debts immediately he was going to invest in property, and that very week was going to look at one with his new partner. He seemed very happy and when I asked him if he loved his life more now than he did before, he replied, "Definitely!" He had brought about the life he wished for by tuning into his heart, then designing a life based on what his heart could tell him. And finally, and most importantly, he got out there and made it happen!

12

GUIDE TO SUCCESS

"Success is getting what you want; happiness is wanting what you get."
Dale Carnegie

"Success is to be measured not so much by the position that one has reached in life, as by the obstacles one has overcome trying to succeed."
Booker T. Washington

"One's best success comes after one's greatest disappointments."
Henry Ward Beecher

"You just can't have big dreams and not go for them"
David Blaine

Learning From Others

THERE are those who have gone before us and left a legacy of power, love and benevolence. We can learn from these people exactly how they made their lives into a living example of satisfaction, kindness and passion. Do you know of people, both living and dead, who inspire you? If not, it is time to get to know some of these people by meeting them or reading about them. The premise of this chapter is:

If someone has done something, then you can learn from them how to do that yourself.

Likewise, if someone lives in a certain way, you can learn from them how to be that way too.

In other words, you can learn from another exactly what they do, and how they do it. Through working with successful people over the years, I have found that they share a common thread to their way of doing things and of being in the world. When you find out how they do these things, you start an amazing process whereby you can do those same things for the same results. This process is an amazing way of transforming your life very rapidly. Instead of reinventing the wheel, you can learn how these people have accomplished what they have. Then you can learn the skills and behaviors that they used to get to where they are. This means that you can be on the constant lookout for qualities in another that you desire for yourself. Instead of being jealous or envious of successful people, you can become curious and inquisitive while you find out exactly what makes them the way they are.

I do this, especially when I am around someone who has aged healthily, or who has plenty of money, or who laughs and smiles a lot. I ask them questions and find out what makes them tick, how they do things, what they say to others, how they feel inside, and anything else that holds the key to their natural behavior. This chapter holds the essence of these answers.

Success is an Attitude

Success is very much affected by your *attitude*. Ask yourself: What is the way that I see the world? Do I see opportunities around me? Or do I see obstructions? Do I see balance? Or do I see only problems? Do I see everything as being perfect? Or do I concentrate on all the imperfections?

Your attitude determines your chances of succeeding in personal life. Destiny will only do so much of the work. The rest is up to you. One of the key factors in gaining an attitude that will attract success and satisfy your heart is to maintain a healthy balance of negative and positive awareness. This means you are *realistic*. You see limitation but you are *not* limited by it. You know that all limitation is flexible and is never static. Any perceived limitation can be opened up by sheer determination and courage. In this way, you and your perception of the world can keep growing and expanding.

Everyone has their story to tell. We can all point to problems in our lives. Yet, when we can see those problems as being *our* responsibilities and therefore being *manageable*, then we can begin to *accept* them. We see them as challenges. They become opportunities for growth and learning. We let others take care of their own problems, thereby allowing them the space to grow and become more responsible. We don't have to find a "perfect partner", an imaginary person that has never experienced pain, conflict, difficulty, stress or problems. We know that all others have had their share of misfortune. More importantly we have learnt the skills that allow us to concentrate on the opportunities of life.

Whether you are focused on opportunities or problems, you will find that the world is littered with them. Focus on problems and that is what you will get. Focus on opportunities and you will find that they present themselves to you every minute of every day. You may find opportunities that will advance your life, for example seeing ways of progressing in your career or ways of bringing you into a more harmonious loving relationship. You may find opportunities to give to others for no reason other than enjoying giving. You can actually open up to opportunities so much that they start looking for you. Then the tiny bit of success that was initially sought for turns into a veritable deluge. When this happens, your life will be transformed beyond your imagination.

So, while acknowledging and accepting that the problems of personal life *are* fundamental to success, obsessing about them *is not*. Don't compromise your chances of success early on by giving too much energy to what may go wrong. Give some by all means, but ensure you give at least as much to the positive elements of your heart's path. That way you will end up with a balanced view of what is going on around you. Success is much more likely to be yours when you are grounded in a balance of this sort. You can see your enemies and your allies. You can see the risks and the rewards. You can go forward in life without getting stuck on "what might not work", "what might go wrong", or "why I should not succeed." Instead you can give sufficient energy to "what will work", "what will go right" and "why I deserve to succeed."

Give yourself this positive option and you may find it works wonders very quickly. Remember that your past does not equal your future. Be authentic. Be unique. Be yourself and the rest will follow.

Applying Insights

INSIGHTS are easy to come by. We can have them every day simply by choosing to have them every day. Some insights are very deep and some are rather trivial. Yet, no matter how profound they are, how they affect us is solely down to how much we apply them in our life.

Having an insight is the first step. Many people stop here. Thinking about the insight is useful, and writing it down can be even more so. A few people get this far. However, applying insights means acting on them. It means making changes in your life in order to accommodate them. This is walking your talk. A very small amount of people achieve this. The reason most people shy away from it is that to have an insight and not act on it seems far safer than to have an insight and act on it.

Applying insights changes your life. The growth that comes from applying insights is essential to being a whole person. Growth is the natural way of feeling connected with God. As an adult, your body has done most of its growing. Yet, your awareness has no end to growth. It can continue to expand infinitely during your lifetime. This is the spiritual growth that enlivens your life.

The growth of awareness through the rigorous pursuit of putting insight into action is not only rare, but is revered and remembered when it happens. So many of the human beings that we consider to be great contributors to the world were people who had amazing insights *and* applied them. We would not remember them if they had only thought about their insights. They were ready to sacrifice their own comfort for the sake of truth. They were ready to feel loss, change, newness and growth because the joy of doing so outweighed the pain they felt while getting there.

Attributes of Successful People

When you have recognized your nature to be God, and God is allowed to flow through your heart as love, then success is guaranteed.

When you know this, then success is not dependent on what you accomplish, because what you are is a success. When you live in this way, the experience of being alive feels successful. Then all accomplishments are like a wonderful bonus and a way to play a game with the world you find yourself in. If you have ever played a game of tennis you will know that the experience of playing it is more important than whether you win or lose. However, you still do everything you can to win. By being involved in personal life as a game, you can fully enjoy the wonders of being alive. You can play to win while at the same time knowing the experience of it is more important than the result.

The game is to change your life so as to make it more and more aligned with the joy within your heart. If you attempt to *gain* this joy by changing your career or relationship, it is likely that you will end up with an improved career or relationship but no greater capacity to enjoy it. This capacity for joy is within us. Joy comes from within and flows forth, touching everything around it and creating the experience of enjoyment. If that inner flow is not present, joy will not be there regardless of what the outside is made up of.

The following attributes of personal success have been based on a number of successful people I have been privileged enough to work with. These people have often been flattered when I ask them how they got to be happy, wealthy or healthy. They are usually delighted to reveal what they know about the way they do things. The following attributes can be practiced and applied to tasks, careers, projects, or relationships. They are as follows:

1. Have a clear vision of purpose
2. Know and use what you need
3. When you see an opportunity, use all your resources
4. Concentrate on the experience more than the goal
5. Don't give up
6. Have faith

1. Have a clear vision of purpose

When you become clear what the path of your heart is, you begin to form a new direction for your life. This gives life a purpose that comes directly from your heart. Successful people all have a clear vision of what their life is about, and why they do the things they do. Someone who knows where they are going can go about their life in a determined way. If you do not have a clear vision of your purpose in life then you will struggle to manifest what you love. When you step up and take on a purpose that you truly love then you will have the wind in your sails as you set out from harbor on an exciting new journey. Without a clear purpose, you will flounder on an open sea and may end up anywhere.

It is useful to keep in mind your vision of what you are going to become and what you are going to achieve. This puts you in touch with your intentions. By continually replaying the images and feelings of your future life, you get to embody that life and attract it towards you. Then you need to identify what you need to get you there...

2. *Know and use what you need*

Knowing what you need to accomplish something is essential. For example, you may know you want to buy a new house, but unless you know what you need in order to do this, you will never be able to get it. In my life I have been exactly in this position. I knew I wanted to buy a house but had no idea what I needed to make it happen. I went to an estate agent who told me I needed to find $45,000 as a deposit to put down on the property I wanted. I had debts of $15,000 and an annual income of $10,000. Two years later, I bought a house. I found the money by changing what I was doing with my life. I had a clear vision of buying a house that gave me the purpose to pursue it. Next I found out what I needed to make it happen (money) and I used it in a way that worked (created a new business). If this sounds simple, it is because it is. We can all accomplish almost anything we wish when we have the purpose towards it, the knowledge of what we need, and the action to use what we need. If only ten per cent of the population have a clear vision of where they are going in life, then imagine how few people actually know what they need to get there, and how many fewer people take action to bring that about. You could be looking at less than two per cent of all people. This formula – purpose, knowledge, action – has brought many "ordinary" people into the public spotlight for their achievements in sport, entertainment and business.

When you use only that which is totally necessary to get a result, then you only use strategies that will work. By determining what will work well, you have already eliminated the vast majority of effort.

If you rely only on trial-and-error to find your way, it will take much longer. Identifying what you need to get a result enables you to be patient until you can make that move. This sometimes involves periods of stillness. Which have a potency of their own. From stillness, action is great. When you know what you need, you can do whatever you can to get it. However at those times when you cannot do that, you can instead allow a stillness to be within your sense of purpose. This is the essence of timing. Eventually, nature takes its course, and the time is right is to get what you need. Another hallmark of successful people is their ability to grab an opportunity when they see one …

3. *When you see an opportunity, use your resources*

You have to have a clear vision in order to recognize an opportunity. Having your heart's path clearly imprinted in your mind is that you will understand when an opportunity is close. Imagine a woman wants a new partner, but of a certain kind. She is choosy and rightly so. She wants a man that is intelligent, funny, happy, well paid, and handsome. She has a clear vision of this. Next time she meets a man like this, she will see him as an opportunity. However, if she has no vision of what she really wants, then she will be confused about what constitutes an opportunity and what does not. She may settle for someone that her heart does not desire.

However, spotting opportunities is not enough in itself to be successful. You have to be ready to take an opportunity by doing whatever it takes. This means using your resources to ensure the maximum chance of landing a passing opportunity. This is because you never know what will tip the scales over into success. If you are close to success, you may not know it. One tiny action of strategy can tip the balance and make it yours.

When you start taking opportunities, you will see that they are everywhere, and that you are getting better at speaking up and taking them. After a while, you may be lucky enough to realize that life is, in itself, an opportunity. It is an opportunity to celebrate that you are God. To celebrate in this way, it is essential to have the next attribute of truly successful people …

4. Concentrate on the experience more than the goal

So what is the point of accomplishments? Whenever I ask this question at seminars, the answers invariably come back the same. One person might say a new car would make them feel successful, another might say that their family makes them feel loved, while yet another might tell me that their business success makes them feel secure. It all comes down to how the accomplishment makes an individual feel.

Imagine that each of your goals is a beach on a tropical island. To get to these beaches, you could walk to them. However the terrain is rough and some beaches are inaccessible by foot. The journey is arduous. If you had a boat, the experience of getting to the beaches would be much more comfortable and enjoyable. Since reaching goals does not have to be a painful process and since you will be traveling to many goals in your life, doesn't it make sense to take transport that will take you there quickly and comfortably? If you were to enjoy the journey then you would not have to wait until you reached your destination to feel happy. The journey in itself would be satisfying.

To be truly successful, it is important to concentrate on the experience of reaching the goal, not only on the goal itself. That way you will feel happy and fulfilled as you go for the goal rather than postponing those feelings until you get there. I have met some people that live in huge houses and have plenty of money, yet their relationships with others are not great and they are bitter about what it took to get to where they are. While most would consider these people to be successful, the reality of their lives is that they are not enjoying their accomplishments. That is why it is so important to appreciate the beauty that surrounds you right now in the present moment. Goals are a wonderful way of defining your life and the way you get there will be the way you will be when you arrive.

The future does not really exist. It is a projection of the mind. The present is where we exist, so it is in the present that appreciation and enjoyment of life must begin. Another attribute of successful people is their ability to keep going whatever the odds ...

5. Don't give up

Giving up can obliterate your chances of success. If success does not come immediately, it is often because it will be a very great success when it does come. Small successes come easily yet great successes require persistence.

Giving up is often a resignation that says, "This is too difficult. I will not continue. I give up." If it is too difficult, then make it less difficult for yourself by taking control. Take a break from it and cultivate stillness. Then, when you are re-energized from the resting and have a fresh perspective from the break away from it, go back and persist. If you keep trying the same thing and no amount of persistence will bring you a result, then you must change the strategy you are using. This means that you are using your resources intelligently and effectively. Finally, all success relies on faith..

6. Have faith

Faith in yourself is the greatest worker of miracles.

If you desire a result with an open-hearted passion *and* you are committed to successfully getting that result, then *it will happen.*

This is the magic of authentic faith. It goes deeper than merely beliefs in the mind. While positive mental beliefs can get rid of doubt, true faith has no doubt in the first place. Faith is the "heart's belief". It is a commitment to something simply "being so". It is the indisputable feeling that something *can and will* turn out the way that is desired. So commit, take action, have faith and … it will happen.

Accepting Yourself While Transforming Yourself

LET us take a moment to reflect upon self-improvement contained in this book. Self-improvement is an organic process. It does not follow linear patterns. Rather you will experience success interspersed with failures. Sometimes you take a step back to take three steps forward.

Accepting your present state while at the same time questing for self-improvement is a wonderfully balanced way to go about life. If you try to improve yourself because you don't like yourself now, you will find that the improvement is slow hard-going work. If you love yourself here and now, you can harness the full power of self-improvement. When self-improvement is genuinely a way to become greater and more powerful, and is not a way to destroy an unloved self, then you will be able to use self-improvement much more effectively and efficiently. This is because your energy is focused on the *goal* (improvement) and not on the *past* (your old self).

Accepting yourself will allow you to confidently focus on the future. You will be safe in the knowledge that who you are here and now is valid and great just how it is. Improvement is so much easier for a person that is already great because there is no pressure and no haste to correct "dysfunction". A more empowering attitude toward self-improvement is: "What I have already is good and whatever I have in the future will be even better". When the improvement reaches a saturation point of quality you will become an outstanding example of humanity and you can then let go of being so future-orientated. You can be present and content.

So as you grow in your capacity to be powerful, remember to enjoy it. Be easy on yourself, love yourself and accept yourself. You are improving yourself because you are *already worthy*. Only the strong can admit their weaknesses and become stronger.

The following exercise will assist you to become more aware of how to learn the ways of success from other people. By learning from them, you will equip yourself with a number of tools that can bring the same results to you.

Exercise

Write a list of ten people you admire. They can be living or dead.

For each one, write down the attributes that you admire in them.

Leave this list somewhere you will see it every day. These are going to be the attributes that you are going to nurture by learning new ways of doing things.

Choose three people from your list that you most admire.

Read about each person, either on the Internet, by buying a book, or by lending a book from a library.
While you read about them, continually ask yourself these questions: "How did they live with these qualities? How did they do things? What kind of things did they say? How did they interact with others?" See if you can find any stories that particularly highlight the quality that you admire about them.

Finally, when you have learnt a little about each person, pretend to be each of them for a few hours.

Walk like they would walk, talk like they would talk, do things with the kind of confidence they would do things. By doing this, you actually embody that person and can unconsciously learn the qualities that you admire in them so that those qualities become your own.

QUESTIONS AND ANSWERS

Q: I find that whenever I try to be more like someone else, I lose touch with my heart's desires. This makes me want to close off to how everyone else does things, and just go my own way in life. Since you say that it is important to honor my own uniqueness, what benefit am I going to derive by copying someone else?

A: Your uniqueness is guaranteed. No one can do things exactly the way you do them. Therefore you will not risk your uniqueness by copying others. However, if you are having difficulty holding to your own heart's values while you learn from others then you are probably easily persuaded. To nurture steadfastness when learning from other people, it is very useful to return awareness to your heart both before and after you study another person. You can remind yourself of what you love and what your heart's path is before you read about another person. You can also do this afterwards. The same goes for when you are embodying the person and acting like them. Remember that you are simply learning a skill from them, just like learning how to make a blackberry pie, or how to draw with charcoal. Learning the skills from them that help you become successful is no different. If you get distracted by their interesting lives then stop and come back to your own heart's values. When you have learned how to copy someone else to the extent that you have their skills, you will see more clearly that you cannot lose your uniqueness in this process. All that happens is that you adopt a quality that you admire in them. The way you adopt this and integrate it into your life is in your own personal way. This exercise is simply a way to avoid reinventing the wheel. When someone in front of you has a skill or personal quality then you can adopt that skill or quality by finding out how they have it and what it is like for them. If you saw someone wearing a coat that you liked the look of, you could find out what shop they bought it from and then buy one yourself. In exactly the same way, you can find out how the qualities of the person manifested in their lives and then do the same to bring it into yours.

Q: I have tried to emulate the success of people around me, especially that of celebrities. I would love to have millions of pounds, a beautiful big house, and to be famous in my work. Yet, this remains a dream. Everything I try just seems to be trite and false. How can I get what those people have?

A: The way to live your dreams can be learned from another. However, you have to bear in mind that while you can learn to do anything that someone else has done, it is going to lead to different results in your own life. This is because you are a different person to them. What you perceive as being valuable is not necessarily what they will perceive as being valuable. You are bound to end up with a different outcome because what you really want to gain is going to be different to what a celebrity wants to gain. So, if you copy the actions of a millionaire, you may get more rich, but not as rich as they are because somewhere, deep down, you don't want to be that rich. If you do want to be that rich and you apply the techniques in this book, then it will happen to you. So, the first thing to find out is what 'inside of you' is stopping you from getting these things. What beliefs are you harboring that say you can't live your dreams? These celebrities you are talking about probably did just what you are doing but without holding onto ways of stopping themselves. They would have looked deep inside themselves and asked what conflicts within were preventing them going forward to their dream life. Doing what they do is not enough. You have to be like they are on the inside also. You have to adopt their attitude, their way of thinking, their connection to the body, whatever is useful to you in replicating their success.

Have the conviction that, whatever it takes, and no matter what may come, you *will* achieve what you want, and it will happen.

Do not for one moment doubt this. Hold strongly to the faith that what is destined will come. Have faith that your destiny is to have your heart's desires manifest in front of your very eyes.

Personal Story

HARRIET had no money when she came to me. She was out of work after barely scraping by as an illustrator and was down in the dumps about life in general. "I just can't seem to get started on anything," she said in a tired voice. "As soon as I start something I want to do something else that seems more interesting." We set to work finding out her priorities in life, which consisted of being with the people that she adored, being physically healthy and having lots of fun. This sounded so good that she started to glow. Then her shoulders slumped. "But how can I get this kind of life and still make money?" I asked her if she knew anyone that had this kind of life. She said that she knew a family friend called Gerri who did. Gerri was always surrounded by friends and children, she was fit and healthy, and she smiled a lot. I asked her to talk to Gerri about what it was that she did to live a life like this, and what it was like to experience it. When she returned to me a week later, Harriet was full of ideas. She had met up with Gerri and Gerri had told her all about her life and how it had changed four years previously. Gerri had been somewhat of a recluse and had been diagnosed with depression. She decided one day that her life was worth more than sitting around feeling miserable all day. So she decided to change it. She did so with the help of a close friend that became a solid source of support and encouragement. Gerri, in effect, had worked out how her close friend lived her life, and to a certain extent copied it to start living a happier life. As Harriet recounted this tale, the penny dropped. "I can do the same thing!" she said.

Three months later, Harriet had a new network of friends and had lost a stone of unwanted fat. She was much more enthusiastic about life. When I asked her about her work and money, the original reason for coming, she surprised me by saying she had she had joined an advertising company and was on a salary of $50,000 a year. We were both overjoyed that she had learnt what she considered to be a successful way to live life. As a direct result of being happy with herself, she attracted people to her and landed a massively improved job and income.

13

Guide to The Work You Love

"Choose a job you love, and you will never have to work a day in your life."
Confucius

"Nothing is really work unless you would rather be doing something else."
Sir James Barrie

"Profit is a by-product of work; happiness is its chief product."
Henry Ford

"I've missed more than 9,000 shots in my career. I've lost more than 300 games. Twenty-six times I've been trusted to take the game-winning shot and missed. I've failed over and over and over again in my life... And that is why I succeed."
Michael Jordan

LOOKING INSIDE

IF you are discontented at work or simply want more from it, then this chapter is for you. It is possible to have to do work that allows you to fully express yourself, be creative and earn lots of money. This chapter shows you how to easily accomplish this.

Yet if it is so easy, why doesn't everybody do it? In my experience, people have two main blocks to fully expressing who they are at work. The first is confusion and the second is fear. If you are confused about the "big questions" in your life, then other people will answer them on your behalf, often for their own gain. These "big questions" include:

- Who am I?
- What is my purpose?
- What do I love to do?
- What is my ideal work?

Take a few moments to answer these questions in an inspiring way. Being unclear about the answers is not an option in a fulfilled life. You will never experience your existence to the full until:

1. These questions disappear because you are living an authentic life; or
2. You answer them yourself from within.

It is helpful to your evolution to ask these questions but it is even more helpful to arrive at one of the two resolutions described above. Great breakthroughs in human evolution occur when someone follows their true inner desires without being constrained by the societal norm. If you work in a job without delving deep into an enquiry of your life, then you will end up doing random work, earning random amounts of money and experiencing a random amount of satisfaction. If you are lucky, you may end up enjoying your job, and earning lots of money. However, if you are unlucky, you can end up with a job you hate, and with money that does not seem to do your work justice. Do you know anyone who is in this situation? It is tough, and entirely unnecessary.

There is a way to guarantee doing the kind of work you love. It is the key to fulfillment in work, and it is really very simple:

Ask yourself what work you want to do and then take steps to make it a reality in your life.

You have the power to create your individual life. Far more is in your control than you may at first realize. If you don't want to work the way you are working, then you can change it.

The second obstacle to doing work that you truly love is *fear*. To be authentic, you must take risks. At first, it seems like there is so much to lose by being authentic. However, by gradually taking the risk of sharing your innermost desires with the world, you will free up your of expression and show your true self. To be authentic means to surrender the obstacles of confusion and fear, and to take the risk of being who you really are. The results are usually very surprising. Far from being rejected or persecuted, you will most likely be accepted, respected and liked for your authenticity. Even those who do not like you will usually at least respect you simply because you are being who you are without excuses. It will then be clear why work is so important to a healthy, balanced life.

Why Work?

Aside from the obvious necessities of food, clothing and shelter, work provides you with the security of discipline and boundaries. It provides a structure within which you can be dynamic and expressive. Your parents or guardians once gave you that structure. They gave you limitations within which you were free to move. If that was done healthily then it kept you from danger while allowing you to explore.

The ability to look after yourself is reflected in your work. A career or a business that you have built up yourself is one of the best ways you can care for yourself. This responsibility is yours and yours alone. In the absence of parental guidance, it is up to you to create discipline and boundaries in your life in a way that suits you. If you set up your career according to the expectations of those around you then you will sacrifice your desires and therefore never fulfill them.

Since, as a person, you are totally unique, you must honor this uniqueness by working in disciplines that your heart desires to work in. Living from the heart is living the life you want. There are five key reasons for doing the work of your heart:

1. Enjoyment
2. Satisfaction
3. Wealth
4. Recognition
5. Contribution

When you enjoy your work, you naturally want to do it. You want to get up in the morning and get going. If you follow the heart, work will be deeply satisfying. Enjoying your work and being satisfied by it means that you will focus on it and excel at it. It is when you are in joy of your work that you will get really good at it. This is because you are massively motivated to do it. Work will no longer seem like a burden to you. A career that suits you down to the ground will be the one that you jump out of bed in the morning for. You will have so much motivation for it that you will give one hundred per cent commitment, dedication, devotion and effort. You will love it so much that you will truly *want* to do it. Wealth comes more easily to people who gain enjoyment and satisfaction from their work. Such people are happy and therefore become a source of inspiration for others. Everyone wants to be inspired and happy. If you create inspiration and happiness for those you work with, you will get promoted. If you create inspiration and happiness for your customers, they will buy from you.

The fourth reason, recognition, gives you a sense of identity. Your work gives you a sense of self as reflected by other people. The feedback other people give you about your work inevitably shapes your work and how you feel about it. All the more reason, therefore, to work from the heart, for then the feedback you receive will be on this level.

Last but not least, work is incomplete without contribution. You are here to dance the light of God into millions of wonderful patterns. When you control this pattern-making process, you can make something of incredible beauty that has a meaningful impact on the world. Whatever you give, give it not through wanting to get, but for the pure expression of love. You will not believe what will happen to you when you do!

Creating Your Ideal Work

THERE are six steps to creating the kinf of work that is ideal to you:

1. Know what you want from work
2. Find your passion
3. Commit to your passion
4. Brush aside doubts
5. Set your income
6. Act with a sense of purpose

1. Know what you want from work

What does success means to you? Is it earning a certain amount of money? Is it becoming famous? Is it achieving one important career goal? Is it building a successful business? Or is it enjoying your work? Asking these questions will help you identify *why* you want to work.

What distinguishes successful work from unsuccessful work is *fulfillment*. When you feel fulfilled in your work, you are naturally successful. A successful career or business will give you at least as much as you put in. It will invigorate you, teach you and enrich your life. Without these characteristics, your work will simply be unfulfilling no matter how much money you earn or how many people know your name.

Knowing what you want is nearly always the first step to getting it. Try the following exercise to clarify exactly what you want.

Exercise

Copy the following list of work rewards onto a new sheet of paper. Add in any other rewards that you can think of. Then, rearrange the list in order of what is most important to you in your work:

- Enjoyment
- Satisfaction
- Money
- Relationships
- Self-image
- Routine
- Focus
- Challenge
- Security
- Balance
- Expression
- Conflict
- Excitement
- Fascination
- Health

By ordering them, you will learn the reasons why you work and what is important to you. With this kind of clarity, it is much easier to …

2. Find your passion

Finding your passion is basically identifying *what* you want to do. This takes awareness that can be raised by focusing on certain areas of your life. Ask yourself these questions:

1. What do I love to do?
2. What do I most want to get from my work?
3. What would I most like to do if I could choose anything?

These questions point the way to your passion. When you are working in something you are passionate about, you can give fully to that work. You can enjoy it. You can repeat it. And you can therefore become successful in it.

Think back to what it was you loved to do as a young child. Remember how easy it was to have passion for certain things. This is the same feeling that can be unearthed in you right now so that you can become clear about what you want to do.

Having a definite goal for your work is of great importance if you are to follow through in achieving what your heart desires. After all, how are you going to get there if you do not know where "there" is? If you use your personal power, your work is much more likely to go where you wish it to. If you are unsure exactly where you want your work to be, then one other powerful way to clarify your working direction is to try many different kinds of work. Try doing things you think you want. Try doing things you intuit you want. Try doing things you know you want. Also, try doing things you don't want to do. Doing things you don't want to do is sometimes the only way to find out exactly what you do want to do. It can provide you with strong motivation to discover your true work path. A job you dislike can say to you, "This is what you will be doing ten years from now if you don't pluck up the courage and create the career *you know you want*." Through a process of elimination you can recognize exactly what your heart's work is.

You know you are working from the heart by the *feeling* it gives you. If you can imagine joy, rapture, challenge, satisfaction, and love all rolled into one emotion, then this is what you feel in peak moments of working from the heart. Ironically, you are very likely to end up earning more money for something you are truly passionate about than for something that you do only out of a sense of duty.

To check whether a certain type of work is your true passion, ask these questions of it:

1. Does it promote growth in me?
2. Does it satisfy me?
3. Do I love it?
4. Does it contribute something special and unique to the world?

When you have defined one or more passions, either instinctively choose the one you will focus on, or even better combine the passions into one career or business. For example, if your passion is children and management, look at becoming a head teacher or nursery manager. Or, if your passion is cooking and traveling then you could cook on a cruise ship or set up an international chain of restaurants. When you are clear about work that you are truly passionate about, then you can easily …

3. Commit to your passion

Committing to your passion means that once you are sure of your passion, you stick to it. You are able to follow through on it with natural persistence to become truly skilled and at it.

The enthusiasm that comes with doing new work is not always enough to carry that work to its fullest fruition. To ensure success, you have to engage in a routine that you can repeat again and again without getting bored or frustrated. This routine is the structure within which you can actively achieve career or business success.

Take acting, for instance. You must rehearse and learn scripts, then tour and put on performances. With one production, you may achieve a little fame, fortune, enjoyment and success. To maintain that success you have to commit to your future. Therefore, to be a truly successful actor, you must *repeat what you are talented at.*

Remember, anyone can grow talent. It is the ability to *repeatedly share a talent* that separates those who are successful at their work from those who are not. Thus, a routine that you are happy to repeat is essential to a successful career or business.

To feel comfortable committing to your future, you may want to take a look at how much time you are willing to give to it. Time is your most precious resource. Money comes and goes but time just simply goes. Check how you feel about committing time to success in your work by asking the following questions:
1. How many hours am I happy working each day?
2. What working hours suit me best?
3. How often do I need to take breaks? (Within a working day, within a working week, and within a working year).
4. How many days am I happy working in a year?

If you are confident in your commitment to your working future then it is much easier to …

4. Brush aside doubts

Have you ever really, really wanted something only to have a little voice in your head say "you can't," or "you shouldn't"? The root of doubt is fear and if we entertain fear, it can crush passion and leave it hidden for years and years, perhaps never to surface again.

However, doing something you are passionate about is one of least risky things you can do. No matter what the dangers, if you are passionate about your work you will be aware, alert and charged with high-energy which will leave you robust and protected. Doubts that say "don't" are therefore *surplus* protection, and can therefore be ignored. When you don't listen to doubts anymore, then you are free to …

5. Set your income

Working from the heart yields immediate emotional rewards. Fulfilling as these emotional rewards are, we still need to eat and clothe ourselves, so at some stage money must be considered. Although money is surely of secondary importance to enjoyment, it does have a very useful function and more of it can mean more choices in your life.

Right now, decide exactly how much money per year you would love to see returning from your work. Then to achieve that level of income you have to ...

6. Act with a sense of purpose

Along the way, you must learn to assert the goals that you have chosen. This means learning communicating effectively to those around you regarding where you want your work to go. It is important to communicate well with your boss, colleagues, spouse and family. It is fine knowing what you want but it is of no use in the real world if you cannot tell others about it. Tell those around you what you want to do but do not share your goals with those who you know will take away energy or enthusiasm away from them.

Complete the following exercise to plan your ideal working life. Revisit and update this plan regularly.

EXERCISE

Fill in all the blanks:

I wish for my work to be in

(Fill in job title or industry.)

I wish to earn $(£)_____per year.

I wish to be doing this work and earning this amount of money in_____years.

I wish to
_____
_____
_____

as a result of my work. (Fill in what you really want to achieve by doing the work.)

I would love doing it because
_____
_____
_____
_____

(Fill in the rewards that will come back to you.)

I can take the following steps to bring about the above wishes:

This week, I will
_____
_____
_____
_____

(Write down three actions you will do in the next week towards reaching your work goals.)

In the next month, I will
_____
_____
_____

(Write down three actions you will do in the next month towards reaching your work goals.)

In the next year, I will

_____

_____

_____

(Write down three actions you will do in the next year towards reaching your work goals.)

QUESTIONS AND ANSWERS

Q: I have made lots of changes to the way I see my career. I know what kind of work I want to do, and how much I want to earn. However, when it comes down to action, I lack the motivation to get going. How can I get motivated?

A: You have identified "how" you want your career to be, but have you considered "why" you want it to be this way? How can you get motivated if you don't know why you are doing it? To get motivated, you have to clear about why you are going to pursue a certain direction. When you are clear about why you want to do something then the rewards and benefits of accomplishing it will provide natural motivation. For example, imagine you know you want to be a consultant and earn $50,000 a year. Ask yourself *why* you want this. Imagine the answer is self-respect, enough money for holidays, enough money to put the children through university, recognition from your peers, and flexible working hours. These are all things you would love in your life. This provides the fire to get moving and do whatever it takes to get that job. As a result, every time you do something that progresses your career you will be sure of the gain that you will get. Furthermore, you will also have a benchmark by which to measure your success. If you are earning $50,000 a year but are not experiencing self-respect, then you know that you have not yet reached your goal. You then know there is something more to be done. Motivate yourself by writing down why you are going to get the career of your dreams and then imagine yourself in that situation. Imagine what it looks like, how you behave, how you feel, what your body posture is like, and how you talk to people. When you have a vivid representation of what it will be like, this should be enough to kick-start some major motivation to take action. It is the action that counts:

Action makes the difference between a dream and a real-world experience.

Q: I have found that I am accomplishing my goals but I am getting very tired in the process. For example, I am now earning over $60,000 which is very close to my initial goal. I am happy about this but the cost has been enormous. How can I reach my goals and maintain that level of income without exhausting my body?

A: This is a very good question and it is timely that you should ask it. You ought always to listen to your body. Its wisdom is beyond words and it will guide you to a place that is comfortable for you. If it is tired then make concessions for it. After all, your success means nothing if you cannot enjoy it in a healthy body. You have done very well in achieving your aims, however it seems as though your priorities have been mixed up along the way. What is most important to you right now, a happy, healthy body or earning lots of money? When you get clear on this you can make adjustments to your lifestyle so those areas of your life that are *most important* to you can be nurtured and grown. Only you know how important your physical health is to you. You have to decide if it is more or less important than the amount of money you earn. If it is then you must take steps to give more time over for your body. If this means working less then that is what it will take. There is always a way to work less, and in a more relaxed way while earning the same income. You can even do this and earn more. It is down to your attitude. Your view of what is possible in your working life will determine the amount of opportunities to improve it that you can see. For example, if you believe that you can earn twice the money by doing half the hours, then you will start to see ways of being able to do this.

Personal Story

CHERYL was a post office clerk. She detested her job and knew she was destined for bigger and better things. However, she felt bound by repayments on her home mortgage. She couldn't see any way to leave her job and continue earning enough to meet her payments. She looked at me with a look of horror when I mentioned that she could leave the job whenever she wanted. "But I don't have a choice," she said. "Why not?" I asked. "Because of my mortgage," she replied. By talking in this way, we had determined that her mortgage was more important to her than quitting her job. There had to be another alternative. To focus Cheryl on her passion in work, I asked her a series of questions, many of which are included in this chapter. It transpired that she was keen to keep doing public service work but that she didn't want to be tied to a desk. We explored her options and she revealed that since a child she had wanted to work in the hotel business. During our coaching relationship she got work as a personal assistant to a hotel manager. The money was slightly better than her previous job but not by much. However, eighteen months later, as a result of her enthusiasm and commitment to improving her working life, she was made manager of a small hotel in the same town. She was delighted as the pay was almost double her previous salary. In less than two years she had doubled her salary and found work that satisfied her. By getting clear about what she wanted and why, she had a vision to work towards. She also did the most important thing: she took action!

14

Guide to an Empowering Relationship

"Love like your life depends on it ... because it does."
Michael Franti

"Friendship is a single soul dwelling in two bodies"
Aristotle

"Always do what you say you are going to do. It is the glue and fiber that binds successful relationships."
Jeffry A. Timmons

"We have stopped for a moment to encounter each other. To meet, to love, to share. It is a precious moment, but it is transient. It is a little parentheses in eternity. If we share with caring, lightheartedness, and love, we will create abundance and joy for each other, and this moment will have been worthwhile."
Deepak Chopra

Unity in Relationships

IT is a wonderful thing to know that you are whole. It means that you do not need to use other people to gain a sense of wholeness. When your relationships are based not on making up a lack but rather on a coming together in celebration then very empowering relationships are possible. If there is no longer a need to fill a lack of wholeness by diving into someone else's life, then you can stand side by side with a partner in a beautifully empowering connection. When you both have an inner temple in which to belong, you do not need each other for the experience of belonging.

In this chapter, we will explore what it means to manifest an empowering relationship and how to do it. At the core of manifesting an empowering relationship, as with the rest of this book, is the experience of God.

Eight Steps to a Satisfying Relationship

A loving relationship is a very energizing, intense, exciting and challenging aspect of human life. It is also one of the least understood. So many unconscious choices go into choosing a mate that it is no wonder that there is so much confusion about how or why we end up in relationships. The kind of people you grew up around as a child will have a very big influence on the kind of partner you choose and the kind of relationship you will have. Every person and couple that you come into contact with will shape your idea of what it means to engage in a loving relationship. This is a good reason to choose your influences carefully from now on

You can become free of the influences of the past by defining for *yourself* who you want to be with and how you want to relate with them. This means that you can choose how to experience relationships and what relationships mean to you. This chapter shows how this can be achieved. It also looks at how you can become more conscious of your relationships, thereby empowering yourself. The ability to merge then separate from a lover is one of the keys to a successful relationship, so this chapter explores how you can steadfastly be yourself in the midst of an intense relationship with a partner.

There are eight steps that you can take to promote full and healthy relationships in your life. The eight steps are:

1. Be clear about what you want
2. Change yourself, not the other
3. Celebrate the differences and the similarities
4. Grow positively without the need for perfection
5. Know when to leave or stay
6. Meet your needs
7. Be yourself while staying devoted
8. Connect with your sexual energy

Taking these steps will bring you improved relationships that are more honest, open and enjoyable.

1. Be clear about what you want

It is essential to know what it is you want from a relationship. Knowing what you want gives you the goals that guide you towards satisfaction.

To realize what you want in a relationship, you have to be still and silent enough to tune in to the silent voice of your heart. The voice of your heart speaks to you in silence, and you can hear it more clearly when you are silent yourself. This means experiencing God without intrusion from activity, thought or communication. With such an experience, the desires of your heart can be seen in absolute clarity. All questions regarding your deepest desires will be answered by the energy that emanates directly from this space of silence.

2. Change yourself, not the other

The result of trying to change someone else is conflict. Conflict arises when you try to change someone else because of one or more of the following reasons:
- They resent the change.
- They become suspicious of being manipulated.
- You do not succeed because they cannot become what you want them to be even if they themselves want it.
- They feel disrespected.
- They feel unaccepted.

The key to changing a relationship for the better is to change *yourself*. Although there are two people in a relationship, it can be dramatically improved by a positive change on only one side. It is far easier to change your own attitude and behavior than another's. A pleasant result of such self-work is that it offers the opportunity for the other to change as well.

The easiest and most effective way to change your relationship for the better is to change your behavior in the areas that you want improvement. For example, if you want your sex life to improve, then personal improvements in your own sexuality will carry over into the sex life of your relationship. Similarly, if you wish for less emotional conflict in your relationship, then letting go of emotions that you don't need anymore is the best way of alleviating that conflict with your partner. As you improve, so does your relationship.

When you have committed to improving yourself, then you can rest contented that you have done all you can. It is then very clear if this is a relationship that will empower you. If your partner wishes you to help them change, then they will ask for your assistance. Helping someone to change can only happen when they are ready and willing for it.

You and your partner may want to make big changes away from each other. When we undertake big changes in our lives, it is sometimes useful to be away from the routines that keep us stuck in unwanted habits. Just as a caterpillar withdraws from the world into its cocoon to emerge later as a butterfly, you can find a space for yourself in which to make radical improvement to the way you behave in a relationship.

When you learn to make desired changes in yourself, your relationships begin to improve. The constriction of conflict gives way to the openness of acceptance. It is in acceptance that relationships flourish and grow.

3. Celebrate the differences and the similarities

Though it is our similarities that draw us together, it is our differences that make us unique. Our differences keep us individual. This is of great importance to our health in relationships. If your partner was exactly the same as you, you would experience total compatibility. It would be as if you were having a relationship with yourself! Without differences there is no sense of sharing. Without differences, there would be no opportunity to learn something new from the other. These differences keep a relationship alive.

EXERCISE

List ten things that you like about your partner that you also like about yourself.

Now list ten things that you like about your partner that have no similarity to you.

Notice how your partner would not be who they were if they did not have the differences you have listed.

Choose one common aspect that you like in yourself and in the other.

Make a date with your partner to celebrate that common aspect. Do it in the same way you would celebrate a birthday or getting a new job. Go all at for a celebration, for example bake a cake, go to restaurant or invite friends around for a party.

Such likeable aspects are the most obvious cause for celebration in a relationship. In celebration, all obstructions to love are dissolved. It can flow between you and your partner freely. Your hearts are open. The experience is of joy. Deep intimacy comes naturally. This is why celebration is an essential part of any couple's relationship. It bonds and reaffirms the positive aspects of sharing and it can rejuvenate a long-standing relationship.

The free flow of love is the key to rich relationships. Celebration is a lubricant of love, easing the passage of love from one heart to another. Celebration stimulates acts of love, which in turn promotes trust between two people.

Celebration is *love* in action.

Such a tangible sign of love is often all that is needed in a relationship that is flagging or cooling off. Sometimes it is easy to forget that love is there. It often needs to be seen or heard, to be believed.

Empower yourself with the ability to create situations in which love is readily expressed. Be in touch with your heart. Celebrate both the common aspects and the differences in your relationship and enjoy the harmony, bonding and intimacy that it produces. Shared celebrations are a special time set aside in relationships for all that is positive. The more conscious celebration there is in a relationship, the more fulfilling it will be.

4. *Grow positively without the need for perfection*

While the attainment of perfection can be very motivating, it is dangerous if you get too caught up in it. With perfection as an aspiration, every achievement appears to be a failure. Perfection is only a concept. It exists no more than imperfection does. If you hold to perfection as being the only satisfying outcome, then life will always seem to be lacking. In relationships, this means that you cannot have satisfaction until a perfect ideal has been achieved. However, it is possible to be satisfied in a relationship that does not match a perfect ideal.

Enjoyment of a relationship is what makes it satisfying. Be wary of using your ideals to postpone your enjoyment of a relationship. Use these instead as goals to direct your growth. You can then seek improvement in your relationship without that improvement undermining the relationship.

5. *Know when to leave or stay*

Perseverance can prove fruitful in relationships. If you turn your back on a relationship as soon as it becomes challenging, then you will limit yourself to a series of shallow encounters. If you persevere and hold the values of honesty, respect and trust high, then nearly all challenges can be overcome. But what happens when this is not the case? What if a certain difficulty persists and no amount of love or awareness makes any difference? It is at these times that you have to gauge the appropriateness of your relationship. To do this, ask these questions: Why am I in this relationship? Is this relationship encouraging my growth? Can I be who I really am in this relationship?

Knowing the appropriateness of your involvement in a relationship will guide you when it comes to the big decision: Shall I stay or shall I leave? By leaving, I mean leaving physical, emotional and sexual interaction. We do not ever totally leave relationships, for they leave an indelible mark on us. The decision is whether or not the mark you are receiving from your present relationship is one that you want to carry for the rest of your life.

To get a harmonious result, choices about relationships must come from the heart. You can tune into the heart through the mind, by being silent and concentrating on what it is that you love. Give yourself some time to be quiet and let your mind run free. Let any thoughts come, but focus on the silence. Let that be your guide. Your heart speaks in silence, so listen to the depths of it by being similarly silent.

6. Meet your needs

Some needs are shallow and some are deep. The shallow needs are often the ones that you might think are important, but really the deep ones are. For example you might feel like you need an alcoholic drink, but really you need to relax. Or you feel like you need a new job, when you actually just need to appreciate the job you already have.

EXERCISE

Write a list of all the things you believe you need.

Do the exercise in Chapter 1 to connect you to God.

Next, look at the list you have written. Take each need in turn and ask yourself the following questions: Do I really need this? Is it a deep need?

Find out what it is that you really need. Find your deep needs.

Then, fulfill the deep needs in your life.

The best way of meeting deep needs is to meet all those that you can meet yourself, and then ask others to do the rest for you. If you look too heavily to others to meet your deep needs, you will give away your power to them. You will become dependent. However, if you stubbornly refuse support in getting your deep needs met, then you will become isolated from others and fearful of intimacy with them. There must be a balance of independence and support to meet your deep needs. Of course, most of the work is up to you since it is your life.

The most common reason that people leave relationships is that their deep needs are not getting met. Even if their partner is meeting their shallow needs, it does not feel fulfilling, as the deep needs are not getting met. If you are in a relationship where all your shallow needs are being met, but there is a lack of satisfaction, it is because your deep needs are being neglected. Rather than facing your deep needs, leaving a relationship can seem like an easier alternative. It is only avoidance however, and the same problem will resurface in any future relationships.

The longer you neglect your deep needs, the scarier it is to allow them to be seen. Deep needs will always manifest as shallow needs until there is enough truth to face them head on. Check whether you are actually in touch with your deep needs before you blame a relationship for not meeting them.

All a need asks for is to be met and accepted. When a need is met and accepted rather than shunned and hidden, then it becomes a part of your life. When a deep need is an accepted part of your life, you will naturally build a life that fulfills it. This is the source of satisfaction in life: knowing your deepest needs, and fulfilling them.

To find out what your deep needs are, it is essential to tune into God. When you know your deep needs, you know whether or not your relationship supports you in meeting them. If your relationship supports you in fulfilling your deep needs thereby aiding you to realize your potential, then it is worth being in.

7. Be yourself while staying devoted

To be truly intimate in a relationship, you must open up to the other. This means temporarily allowing your emotional and physical boundaries to dissolve. When this happens, you can merge into your partner and experience the whole of them. When this emotional and physical merging with your partner is over, your boundaries must reform for you to retain your sense of self. If you are not adept at reforming your boundaries, the cost of this merging is to lose your individuality. You may feel overwhelmed by the relationship as if you cannot be yourself in it.

How can you be yourself in a relationship while staying totally devoted to the other? There is a fine balance between self-nurture and devotion to another. If you get obsessed with self-nurture then you get too isolated to enjoy a relationship. However if you get lost in another person's life, you forget how to respect our own desires. To tread the balance, you must steadfastly follow your own heart's path while at the same time remaining devoted to your partner.

When it is clear what your heart's direction is in terms of career, relationship style, sexuality, choice of home, social interaction, physical exercise, leisure, diet and creativity, then you will have a strong individual path. You can then devote yourself to another in a relationship without compromising your dreams, your desires or your sense of identity. This is the only way for a sustainable relationship to remain harmonious. Without a strong individual path, merging into another can lead to a neglect of your deepest needs. The conflict of wanting the intimacy of devotion and yet having to compromise one's own natural path to do so is undesirable.

When you are assured of your unique individual nature then you know who you are, what you want out of life and where you are heading. The influence of a loving partner can then be welcomed instead of being resented. If you are sure of where it is that you are going, then you do not need to fear any detours that you may take in order to meet another who is going in a different direction. If you do not know where we are going, such a detour may distract you from your path.

If you accept the differences between you and your partner then the need to be the same people is not there. It is the recognition of your nature as God that will feed you with wholeness. When you have the recognition that you are God then you do not need to make up for a lack of wholeness by being in a relationship. You can accept each other's differences and devote yourselves to one another without a need for your personalities and interests to conform. Such acceptance is a key to sustainable intimate relationships.

8. Connect with your sexual energy

Sexual energy is at the core of your personality. When you have congruency between your sexual energy, and your thoughts, feelings and expressions, then you will feel more contented. This means that when you feel sexual, and the sex energy is rising in your body, your mind accepts it, your emotions give it space, and your expression supports it. Sexual energy is the very life force that created your body in the first place. Therefore experiencing it is a great opportunity to *connected with your body.*

Being connected to your body in the sexual experience is something that will encourage your mind, emotions and expressions to align with the sexual energy. When your body is plugged in and fully connected to the pulsating sexual current running through it, then the sexual experience is *immediate*. It is not abstracted or ignored but rather is immediately present and available to you.

With sexual experience being *immediate*, the mind does not need to imagine sexuality. Instead, it can think of what is occurring right here, right now. When you are present with the sexual current in your body, then your feelings will give sexual current space. Emotions such as fear, anger or sadness can suppress sexual instinct, making it stagnant or mischievous. Tuning into your sexual energy by letting it connect with you in your body automatically gives sexual energy more power of expression.

When sexual energy is *immediate* in your body, then your expression of that energy can be direct and honest. You do not need to hide it, or be scared or embarrassed of it. Sexual energy created your body. The energy can of course be expressed in sexual intercourse but if that is either impractical or undesirable then the very same energy can be used as a source of power and motivation. It can be used in an infinite number of ways including business, art, sport, fitness, bodybuilding, music, work, finances, meditation or dance.

When you have congruency between your sexual energy and your thoughts, feelings and expressions of it, you have empowered yourself to be *who you are as a sexual being*. You will give yourself the wonderful opportunity of expressing sexual energy in your life in a positive, growth-promoting way.

Try the following exercise to get clear about your dream relationship

Exercise

Write down your dream relationship. Make a list that describes it. Include the qualities of the other person, the kind of interaction you envisage, and how you would feel about the relationship. Include all your desires, fantasies, dreams and hopes, no matter how far-fetched they may seem.

Now ask yourself these questions for each description: How would I feel about this? What would the consequences of this be? Am I ready for it now? If I am not ready for it, what changes do I need to make in order to be ready?

Next, take the first steps towards making the changes you need to. Do this now!

Look back on what you have written in about one month's time. You will be able to see how much has actually manifested in your life.

Questions and Answers

Q: I am living with my partner and I am becoming very nervous. I think he wants to marry me. I love him dearly, yet feel too scared to commit to him. What can I do?

A: This is a very common occurrence in meaningful relationships. Commitment can be a scary experience, because when you commit to something, you tend to grow. This growth has an unknown element to it. You may be wondering, "What am I going to become if I commit to this?" Hence there is fear. However, rather than jeopardizing a beautiful relationship by being led by the fear, you can instead befriend the fear. While this may sound odd, befriending fear is simply accepting that the fear is there and that it is part of you. The problem with not accepting that the fear is part you is that it can control your life. If it is part of you then you are bigger than the fear. Then you are able to move from the heart. This means you get along with those "nervous" or "scary" feelings but move towards what you love, regardless. The results of doing this are extraordinary!

Q: You often talk about "the heart". Sometimes I am confused by what my heart's direction actually is. How do I recognize the difference between my heart and my thoughts?

A: The quieter you can be, the more you will hear your heart. I don't mean that the mind has to stop talking, just that you can be quiet enough in the activity of "doing the mind" so that you are not conjuring up more thoughts.

If *you* can stay quiet even when your mind is active, then the voice of the heart can be heard more clearly.

One of the easiest ways to do this is to see a reflection of your heart's voice. This means noticing what your responses are when you do something. If you feel a deep sense of satisfaction and enjoyment then you have moved spontaneously from your heart. When that happens in your life, you can see that, "This was a movement from my heart." Next time around, you will be able to distinguish more and more what is the heart and what is the mind.

Personal Story

PATRICIA is a housing officer with the council. She had been in a number of relationships where she was very attracted to a man but felt terrified at the same time. Each time she would inevitably back out of the relationship in fear. This had happened to her four times in the last five years, each time with men that she really wanted to be with. When she came to me, she was in complete desperation. "What can I do to stop this feeling of fear?" she asked. In my experience, this is the most common type of relationship problem. Fear arises from a person's past and seems to haunt them. They cannot commit to a relationship at the point when it is vital to do so, so they end up leaving it although they would rather stay. I knew that Patricia, like all people, had the ability to face her fears and do what she wanted to do regardless of them. I found out how she did this in other areas of her life by asking her about a time she had experienced overcoming a scary challenge in the past. She remembered her driving test. I got her to remember it very vividly so that she could feel the same emotions that she experienced back then. Her face changed. She looked determined. While she was in this state, I started talking about her current relationship, occasionally using little metaphors based on her driving test like "I bet that was a good test," and, "I am sure it is possible to feel like you are in the driving seat."

Meanwhile, she was subconsciously making associations between her ability to face fears and her current relationship.

Three weeks later she called me, "Thanks so much. I feel so settled and confident about this relationship now. I don't feel the need to run away from it any more." Patricia had displayed the ability that we all have to take the skill of overcoming fear from one area of our life and then apply it to another area.

15

GUIDE TO CREATING ABUNDANCE IN YOUR LIFE

"The resource from which God gives is boundless, measureless, unlimited, unending, abundant, almighty, and eternal.
Jack Hayford

"I have learned this at least by my experiment: that if one advances confidently in the direction of his dreams, and endeavors to live the life which he has imagined, he will meet with a success unexpected in common hours."
Henry David Thoreau

"The great end of life is not knowledge but action."
Thomas H. Huxley

"Life is too short to be little."
Benjamin Disraeli

BE GOD

AT the very heart of your being, there is only God. When you become more and more acquainted with returning to your heart then you will experience a unified state. When God is your nature then it cannot be taken from you. Nor can it be bought, traded, lost or found. Then eternal peace is guaranteed. The mystery of life is to awaken to the grand splendor of this, your own wholeness. When you accept fully that you are whole, the mystery vanishes, and you are left with a life that is wide open – one that you yourself can shape with your heart as the leader.

Remember that it is only when your heart leads your life that you are guaranteed to fully experience God in the world around you. I have faith that this book will have kick-started an unstoppable transformation within you that will allow you to prosper on all levels, and experience the full vividness of this amazing phenomena we call existence.

As a parting gift, I wish to explain the basic principles of magic. Magic has been painted with quite a dark brush by some people on our planet, however it is only a means to manifest things or experiences. This being so, we are responsible for creating magic every day and it need not be feared. However, when we more fully understand the structure of the force behind manifestation, then we can tailor it to align with our hearts desires. Thus, we step into the experience of deepest satisfaction.

It is only when we experience the infinite vastness and beauty of God within us that we realize how very precious life is. The human form is a conduit for the power of love to flow forth from the stillness of God into the motion of action. When we recognize this fully in a very real and practical way then talking about it and questioning it becomes merely a pastime. We can step up into a life that continually reveals the natural beauty that lies within. But to reach this state of passionate power, we have to manifest things in our life according to what we know of God deep inside us. This means creating magic according to the heart. After all, the heart is the gateway between our human form and God. To become truly balanced individuals, our personal lives have to be lived from the heart in a massively powerful way. This power becomes focused and concentrated in a beneficial way using the techniques in this chapter.

Designing Your Life

AS you are acting to make your dream life come true, continue to go to the source of all life – that stillness inside of you that is God. By allowing God to have full access to your personal life, you will inevitably receive abundant benefits.

To be on the outside as you are on the inside requires you to become aware of the immense power of your own situation. You are the only thoroughly consistent factor of your life, so it is down to you to adapt your life so that is more congruent with the power, beauty and ease that resides within your depths.

It is important to know the secret of magical manifestation:

When you act with a sense of inevitability, you attract towards you that which your heart desires.

This means that having a direct experience of what something is like before you actually see, hear or feel it in the outside world actually assists in that thing becoming present. This is so for two reasons, firstly:

When you see, hear and feel internally what something will be like, you program your mind, body and emotions to identify opportunities for its manifestation.

This readies you for what you would love to have in your life. For example, if you know what your ideal career is like then you will be able to spot the career opportunities that will lead to that. Those opportunities may be in front of you right now. Knowing in your mind, body and emotions what you want means that you can spot it when it is there. This is a case of knowledge being power. The trick is to know what you love in very fine detail so that you actually have a clear memory of experiencing it (even though it only happened internally). This then tunes you in to the actions that need to be taken towards its manifestation. The beauty of this is that while you take action, the parts of your mind, body and emotions that are unconscious (which is most of them) are working on your behalf to produce the results you love. This is true congruency in action.

Hold in your mind the result you wish to attain while you act to attain it. By doing so, you will program yourself to act as if it is has already happened. This will massively multiply your ability to accomplish it. While acting to make your dream life, keep coming into an awareness of who you are. Make sure you let your awareness move beyond your personal life so that you have no doubt that you are also God.

The second reason that acting with a sense of inevitability attracts what your heart desires is:

When you experience what you would love to happen as an experience right here and now, then you impress it upon God's infinite potential.

In God, all things are possible. All things are potential and waiting to happen. When we have a direct experience of what we would love to happen, *and* experience that as happening right now in this very moment, then we are effectively appreciating the infinite resources of God. In doing so, we impress our wish upon God and we are provided with the fulfillment of that wish. The way this happens is beyond our control but *it does happen*. I have witnessed hundreds of such incidences in both myself and others. The way I explain it is this: You are God, the one spirit. God is at the very core of who you are. If you were to travel inwards from your personal self, all that would remain is pure God, a formless, nameless, unified spirit. God is the wellspring of all things. Since that wellspring is who you are, then asking it to fulfill a wish is no different from the mind asking your body to do something, followed by the body doing what was requested of it. You are merely asking a part of yourself to do what it does, and it responds by doing it. Of course you cannot absolutely control how your wish gets fulfilled, just like the mind cannot absolutely control the body. However, by implementing the exercise in this chapter, you will get very close to total control.

EXERCISE

Centre yourself by taking five minutes to sit somewhere comfortably. Close your eyes and relax.

If you can feel any tension in the body, clench all the muscles in the part that is tense and then relax that area completely.

Next, become clear about God within you. Notice how the breath flows by itself. Follow the breath to its source to find that you are totally whole.

Now allow your heart to define for you what you would love most in your life right now. Get that intention very clearly. For example, you may wish for a healthy body, or a million pounds.

Now put yourself into the "End State". Do this by visualizing the scenario so that you are in it now. Hear, feel and see what it is like there. How do you move? What is your body posture like? How do you talk to people? What do you feel in your body? What can you see? Are the colors vivid? Can you see a tremendous amount of detail? What can you hear? Is it loud or quiet? Is it pleasant?

While you imagine that you are there, imagine that there are now two of you: there is a "future you" that is the one in the End State, and there is a "past you" that is the one sitting with closed eyes doing this exercise right now. Embody the "future you" and start talking out loud to the 'past you'. Tell the "past you" all the things that must be done in order to reach the End State that the "future you" is in. This can take the form of a dialogue between the "future you" and the "past you". Being specific is important here. Rather than "Improve my diet," be more specific. Describe specific actions that are doable by you, for example, "Increase my intake of Essential Fatty Acids," or "Book a session with a renowned nutritionist."

When the instructions have been clearly passed from the "future you" to the "past you", open your eyes, and write down all the actions that were given to you.

The last step is essential: Carry out these actions while encompassing the End State. This means doing all the actions that were suggested *and* doing them while you imagine the End State. So if the intention was to have a healthy body, the End State experience might have been the vision and feeling of running in a field laughing. One of the instructions may have been to book a session with a nutritionist. Before you make the call, and just before you turn up for the appointment, go to the End State experience again. Close your eyes and go back to that vision and feeling of running in a field.

Questions and Answers

Q: I have tried the technique and it didn't work. I wanted to get enough money to buy a car in the next month. I did what you said. I visualized it and told the "me" in the present what to do next. Then I went to do it. I knew at the time that it was unlikely to work, and I was proved right. I have got into debt this month, quite the opposite of what I had wished. What could I do differently?

A: The actions toward your wish are vital but it is very important to experience the End State while you carry out the actions. Remember that you do something knowing that it will not work then you will negatively influence the chances of it working. It may work despite that attitude, but it is definitely less likely to. To ensure successful results, it is essential to carry out the actions with the End State present in your mind, body and emotions. If I met you after a football match that your team had won, you would no doubt be jubilant and energized. Even though the game was over, the feelings and thoughts of it would still linger. This would definitely affect who you are and how you behave, which we all know is very important. Entering the End State is exactly the same idea. Stepping into the End State before doing the action will give you a sense that it will definitely happen, which then attracts that result right to you. Act as if it has already happened. Try it again in this new way.

Q: I love the idea that we can magically make things from the universe. However, I have problems imagining the "End State". First of all, I have difficulty visualizing it then I think that I must have chosen something out of my league. Then I guess I just give up. Am I doing it wrong?

A: Well, I wouldn't call it wrong exactly. There are two points I would like to make. Firstly, not everyone visualizes an internal experience easily. So, go easy on yourself. If pictures do not come, then you are not "wrong". You can use the other senses of hearing and touch instead. Imagine the feeling you would have, both the emotions and the physical sensations. Imagine the sounds you might hear. Even one sense is enough to evoke the End State so you could use only sound or only touch. Remember that this is about you stepping into your capacity to create magic in your life. It will therefore happen in your own unique way. The second thing to bear in mind is that by its very nature, your End State will have to be out of your league. If you do not choose something that is seemingly beyond you then you will stick to something that is so close to your present abilities that this exercise is hardly worthwhile. To get amazing results, imagine amazing transformations and then step into the End State. Find out what you have to do right now to bring it about, then go and do it while experiencing the End State. I have seen this method transform the lives of people. Some people make a lot of money, others find their soul mate, and others start a job that they are truly passionate about. People that live a life they truly love do so by being clear about what is going to manifest in their life before it actually does. They are able to see and experience things that are not already there. In effect, they tune into the vast reservoir of potential within God and interact with it in a way that personalizes the creation process.

PERSONAL STORY

WHEN Eric came to me, he explained that times were very tough. Having been divorced five years previously, he felt that his best days were over. He was broke and lonely. When I asked him what he would most like to change about his life, he told me he wanted financial security and a large group of friends that he loved to be with. When I asked about his current financial and social situations, he said that he was never any good at making money, neither could he hold on to it if he did. He also said that although he knew many people, he did not consider them friends, and added wryly that he did not like any of them! It was clear to me that Eric's own attitude was the main component in preventing his wishes coming true. His did not lack skills as far as I could see, nor did he present himself as an antisocial character. To begin with, I showed him how he could centre himself by sitting with closed eyes and concentrating on his breathing. He found this profoundly relaxing, and did it many times during the first week of coaching. Then I asked him to imagine himself in the situation he wanted to be in, with abundant money and a great group of friends. I got him to visualize nearly twenty different scenes where he was interacting with plenty of money and spending quality time with friends. Once he was really seeing, hearing and feeling his own behavior in those scenes, I could see his body posture changing. He was smiling broadly. I asked him to imagine himself looking back at the "past Eric" and see him sitting in the room where we were doing the exercise. He said he was doing just that. He started to laugh. When I asked him what was so funny, he told me that the "past Eric" seemed so naïve, as if he was pretending to be content with what he had, but deep down was dissatisfied with life. I asked him to coach the "past Eric" and tell him what needed to happen so that his future life (the one of abundant money and friends) could be achieved. After about fifteen minutes, Eric had briefed himself on what needed to be done. During the following three months, he carried out the suggested actions, ensuring that each one was done in the End State. He was thrilled when I saw him after about five months. In that time, he had increased his income from $18,000 to $38,000, had a new circle of friends that he talked passionately about, and had met a special lady that had obviously touched his heart. He said something that I'll never forget: "Choosing my lifestyle has been like ordering from a menu in a restaurant. I used to do order something I didn't really want just because I was scared and worried. Now I have ordered the dish I want most, and it is so satisfying!" Eric had applied the golden principle of self-coaching from the End State and entering it again while carrying out the suggested actions. God was able to express directly through his heart as he went about building the life he loves. His mind and body were programmed with the sense that he was already there, and as such he attracted that to himself.

Epilogue

A Fond Farewell

SINCE the destiny of every man and woman is to tread their own unique path, we are all bonded by God. It is in the very fact that we are so different that makes us all the same. Every person's uniqueness is testimony to the fact that we are not as different as meets the eye. If this sounds paradoxical, it is because it is! We are both unified with one other and distinct from one another. When we stand up and sing our song with all the breath in our bodies, then God is really revealed to be within us. We can all achieve a flowering of our uniqueness that sets us free from the bondage of having to conform or copy one another. It is in our originality that true success and power is found.

I hope you have prospered from reading this humble work, and that you can take some of the skills that have been learnt within these pages forward to benefit yourself and those you love. The more of us that live a life from the heart, the more peace and joy will descend on this troubled and confused planet. Play local, love global. Farewell until we next meet.

Resources

Heart in Action is Conor Patterson's personal development consultancy which includes coaching in sports coaching, nutrition, finance and spirituality.

Heart In Action
PO Box 97
Hove
BN3 5XE
UK
Tel: +44 (0)1273 83 20 83
www.heartinaction.co.uk

The Life Coach Website is where you can find Conor's life coaching work and events:
www.lifecoach.gb.com

Conor's website is a more personal and spiritual site featuring interviews, book extracts and poetry:
www.conorpatterson.com

Win At Sport is Conor Patterson's Sports Performance Coaching site offering an explanation of how it can raise your game:
www.winatsport.com

O

is a symbol of the world,
of oneness and unity. O Books
explores the many paths of wholeness
and spiritual understanding which
different traditions have developed down
the ages. It aims to bring this knowledge
in accessible form, to a general readership,
providing practical spirituality to today's seekers.
For the full list of over 200 titles covering:

- CHILDREN'S PRAYER, NOVELTY AND GIFT BOOKS
- CHILDREN'S CHRISTIAN AND SPIRITUALITY
- CHRISTMAS AND EASTER
- RELIGION/PHILOSOPHY
- SCHOOL TITLES
- ANGELS/CHANNELLING
- HEALING/MEDITATION
- SELF-HELP/RELATIONSHIPS
- ASTROLOGY/NUMEROLOGY
- SPIRITUAL ENQUIRY
- CHRISTIANITY, EVANGELICAL AND LIBERAL/RADICAL
- CURRENT AFFAIRS
- HISTORY/BIOGRAPHY
- INSPIRATIONAL/DEVOTIONAL
- WORLD RELIGIONS/INTERFAITH
- BIOGRAPHY AND FICTION
- BIBLE AND REFERENCE
- SCIENCE/PSYCHOLOGY

Please visit our website,
www.O-books.net

THE WISE FOOL'S GUIDE TO LEADERSHIP
Peter Hawkins

Nasrudin is the archetypal wise fool, who lived in the Middle East over 600 years ago, though his stories have travelled the world and been updated in very generation. *Peter Hawkins* has given a modern spin to 84 of these stories by turning Nasrudin into a management consultant. Simple truths are told in a straightforward and highly entertaining way. They shock us into seeing situations and ideas with which we have become familiar from a different perspective. Each story slips into our house by its engaging good humour, but once inside it can start to rearrange the furniture and knock new windows through the walls of our mind-a process that can be releasing and refreshing, but at times disconcerting!

The book also provides an introduction to Nasrudin and his stories, and a chapter on "Telling Tales; the positive use of stories in organisations."

I commend this book to you-wiser even than The Hitch Hiker's Guide to the Galaxy, *far, far funnier than* In Search of Excellence, *so much thinner than* The Harvard Business Review Encyclopedia of Corporate Strategy, *and astoundingly cheaper than Catch 22!* Professor Mike Pedler

Dr Peter Hawkins is co-founder and Chairman of Bath Consultancy Group, which operates internationally in helping all types of organisations manage change.

1 903816 96 3
£7.99/$11.95

THE 7 AHA!S OF HIGHLY ENLIGHTENED SOULS
Mike George

With thousands of insights now flooding the market place of spiritual development, how do we begin to decide where to start our spiritual journey? What are the right methods? This book strips away the illusions that surround the modern malaise we call stress. In 7 insights, it reminds us of the essence of all the different paths of spiritual wisdom. It succinctly describes what we need to realize in order to create authentic happiness and live with greater contentment. It finishes with the 7 AHA!S, the "eureka moments", the practice of any one of which will profoundly change your life in the most positive way.

Mike George is a spiritual teacher, motivational speaker, retreat leader and management development facilitator. He brings together the three key strands of his millennium-spiritual and emotional intelligence, leadership development, and continuous learning. His previous books include *Discover Inner Peace, Learn to Relax* and *In The Light of Meditation*.

1 903816 31 9
£5.99 $11.95

MASTERING E-MOTIONS
Feeling Our Way Intelligently in Relationships
Richard Whitfield

Human feelings and emotions are the revolving doors to intellect, action and spirit. Guided by the reality that humans are much more driven by their emotions than by the intellect, this book gives readers both insights and know-how for improved personal emotional management.
    Using a clear conceptual structure, the practical emotional growth promoted here can benefit every aspect of life, including intellectual and work performance, personal contentment and quality of relationships.
    The author writes from wide experience, and a deep educational concern for holistic models for human development and functioning. The text takes much of the mystique out of 'emotional intelligence', and, with associated insights from brain science, enables readers both to shape and to 'get a life'.

Central to it are the age-old "golden rule" wisdoms, which are not innate at birth but must be learned and handed on by experience. It offers challenging and practical solutions that require responses in lifestyle and outlook. Then our collective democratic consciousness may awaken to the massive evolutionary risks that we face unless we "mind" our emotions.

Richard Whitfield, Professor Emeritus of Education, is an international lecturer, teacher and consultant. He has previously been University Lecturer at Cambridge, Dean of Social Sciences at Aston University, UK Director of Save the Children Fund, and Warden of St George's House, Windsor Castle.

1 905047 26 6
£11.99 $19.95

HUMMING YOUR WAY TO HAPPINESS
An introduction to Tuva and Overtone singing from around the world
Peter Galgut

Ancient peoples have always used incantations and music to tune into nature and achieve expanded consciousness, better health, and for purposes of divination. The most powerful of all forms of sound healing and transformation is the technique of overtone chant, still practiced in many parts of the world today.

This guide shows you how to calm and focus the mind through singing the ancient way. It draws on sources from around the world, covering Pythagorean, Eastern, Jewish, Christian, American and African musical traditions. It covers ancient beliefs in the Lost Chords, Music of the Spheres, Tantras, Chakras, the Kabbalistic tree as well as modern concepts of white sound, brainwave generation and others. It is full of techniques and tips on how to keep "on top", using sound, music and harmony, helping you to take control of your life in your own way in your own time.

Dr Peter Galgut is a medical scientist and clinician at London University, as well as a qualified Acupuncturist and Homeopath.

1 905047 14 2
£9.99 $16.95

THE QUEST
Joycelin Dawes

What is your sense of soul? Although we may each understand the word differently, we treasure a sense of who we are, what it is to be alive and awareness of an inner experience and connection with "something more." In *The Quest* you explore this sense of soul through a regular practice based on skills of spiritual reflection and be reviewing the story of your life journey, your encounter with spiritual experience and your efforts to live in a sacred way.

Here you become the teller and explorer of your own story. You can find your own answers. You can deepen your spiritual life through the wisdom and insight of the world's religious traditions. You can revisit the building blocks of your beliefs and face the changes in your life. You can look more deeply at wholeness and connection and make your contribution to finding a new and better way.

So well written, constructed and presented, by a small independent group of individuals with many years experience in personal and spiritual growth, education and community, that it is a joy to work with. It is a lifelong companion on the spiritual path and an outstanding achievement; it is a labour of love, created with love to bring more love into our world.
Susanna Michaelis, *Caduceus*

1 903816 93 9
£9.99/$16.95

EVERYDAY BUDDHA
A contemporary rendering of the Buddhist classic, The Dhammapada
Karma Yonten Senge

These quintessential sayings of the Buddha offer a rich tapestry of spiritual teachings and reflections on the spiritual path. More than just a collection of Buddhist sayings, *The Dhammapada's* message is timeless and crosses all cultural boundaries. It offers the reader a constant source of inspiration, reflection and companionship. It is a treasure trove of pure wisdom that has something to offer to everyone.

Everyday Buddha brings the original teaching and traditional text of *The Dhammapada* into our 21st century lifestyle, with a contemporary context. Without straying far from the Pali text it renders it in a fresh and modern idiom, with a universal appeal. An introduction provides a background to the life and times of the historical Buddha, and his teachings on the four noble truths and eight fold noble path.

Foreword by H.H. The Dalai Lama, with his seal of approval.

Karma Yonten Senge is a Dharma practitioner of the Karma Kagyu tradition of Tibetan Buddhism. He is an avid follower of Buddha Dharma, and currently lives in Australia.

1 905047 30 4
£9.99/$19.95